STARTING SCHOOL AT 4

Marion Dowling is an independent specialist in early years. She was formerly an HMI working for OFSTED. In the course of her career she has taught in primary schools, been a nursery headteacher and worked as an advisory headteacher and senior primary adviser. She has contributed to early childhood education inservice courses in many parts of Britain and overseas. As well as publishing articles in professional journals, she is author of *The Modern Nursery* (1974, Longman), *Early Projects* (1978, Longman), co-author of *Teaching 3–9 Year Olds* (1984, Ward Lock), *Talking Together: Language Materials* (1986, Nottingham Education Supplies) and *Education 3–5* (1988, 1992, Paul Chapman Publishing).

STARTING SCHOOL AT 4:

A SHARED ENDEAVOUR

MARION DOWLING

P·C·P
Paul Chapman
Publishing Ltd

Paul Chapman Publishing Ltd
144 Liverpool Road
London
N1 1LA

British Library Cataloguing in Publication Data

Dowling, Marion
  Starting School at Four: Joint Endeavour
  I. Title
  372.241

ISBN 1–85396–270–8

Typeset by Palimpsest Book Production Limited,
Polmont, Stirlingshire
Printed and bound by Athenaeum Press, Gateshead

A B C D E F G H 9 8 7 6 5

CONTENTS

PREFACE

This book has two main intentions: to highlight the issues concerning the first year in school and to consider the needs of 4-year-olds. However, it is not a book which advocates the admission of 4-year-olds to school. In an ideal world these children should be in nursery establishments. The reality, though, is that very many of our young children are already in mainstream schools and that this trend is likely to continue at least in some parts of the country. I also acknowledge the considerable amount of thought and commitment that has gone into much of this provision. In some circumstances our 4-year-olds are benefiting considerably from a shared endeavour.

Nevertheless, we cannot be satisfied with partially good provision. At a time when there is a great deal of uncertainty about the form of education and care for our under-5s it is essential that we distil evident good practice, consider the factors that support that practice and argue strongly for these factors to be a requirement for the future education of all 4-year-olds. The curriculum for this phase of education is not mandatory and so the responsibility for both content and methodology lies with well qualified and able early years practitioners. I have written this in the hope that it will be helpful to them and also as a tribute to their dedicated work.

Grateful thanks as always to my family and friends who have encouraged and advised me.

Marion Dowling

INTRODUCTION

The child's introduction to and early experiences in school are likely powerfully to influence his or her attitudes to learning and subsequent achievements in education. This is well recognised in many schools and results in sensitive and carefully planned practices. However, the introduction of the National Curriculum has turned attention away from the reception class and possibly dulled awareness of the ongoing complexities of the task of the reception teacher. I believe that it is timely to look again at the first year in school in the light of the current educational climate. One major reason for a rethink is the growing tendency to have 4-year-olds in school.

Children are legally required to start school in the term following their fifth birthday, at which age they follow the programmes of study set down for Key Stage 1 (KS1) in the National Curriculum. In reality admission dates vary widely and most children enter school between 4 and 5 years of age. In a recent OFSTED survey of reception classes, 57 per cent of children started school between 4 and 4½ years of age.[1] Moreover, there is now a widespread practice of admitting children once a year only in September, resulting in the youngest entrants being just 4 years, one day. Woodhead predicts that in due course the age for starting school will have become 4 in practice, if not in statute.[2]

The reasons for this move to early admission are a curious combination of political and economic expediency, response to local need and belief in educational benefit.

One factor influencing the move towards admitting 4-year-olds to school was the falling school rolls in the 1970s and the availability of spare classrooms. Although numbers recovered considerably during the 1980s, the upturn was not evenly spread demographically: some inner-city and rural schools still have to seek ways of boosting their numbers and will do so by admitting younger pupils. Even where numbers are relatively stable, the effects of schools having their own budgets and the pressures of competition resulting from open enrolment now cause other schools seriously to consider admitting a non-statutory age-group as one means of securing their school membership.

In taking this action, schools are sometimes tentative about being able to meet the needs of young children with limited resources, but they are aware that they are usually responding to parental wishes. State nursery provision remains thin overall and unevenly spread. The growth of preschool playgroups and private nurseries has meant that this is a real option for many 3- and 4-year-olds, but only for those families who are prepared and able to pay. The demographic spread of playgroups is also uneven, with significantly less provision in the poorer areas of the country. However, even if the government's promise materialises to increase nursery provision for all 4-year-olds, given the choice, many parents are likely to opt for early school entry in the belief that this will give their children a head start to the National Curriculum programmes of study.

There has also been a strong move to have a single admission to school in September as a means of compensating for the recognised disadvantages of summer-born children. Where schools have followed the statutory requirements for admission and admitted children to school within the term in which they become 5, this has resulted in a pattern of three intakes during the year. This admissions policy contrasts with other year-group transitions that, by convention, are on an annual basis in September. Where this policy is followed, children born in the summer months are admitted to the reception class in that term and experience only one term there before transferring to the next year group. At the end of their infant-school career, older autumn-born children will have received eight or nine terms of schooling as compared to the summer-born children who will have had only six or seven terms as an infant. For 25 years now there has been mounting evidence that summer-born children are heavily represented as underachievers. One LEA, for instance, changed its admissions policy to a single point of entry on the basis of this issue being successfully argued.

Under termly admission, summer-born children suffer a dual disadvantage of being both the youngest in a year group throughout their school careers as well as having less schooling. With some children this can have long-term effects. Mortimore's study of junior schools in inner London showed that the younger pupils in classes demonstrated more behavioural difficulties and poorer attainment in reading, writing and mathematics.[3] In addition, children starting school in the spring and summer terms are often required to join an already-established group admitted earlier in the year. Hughes, Pinkerton and Plewis looked at the nature and extent of children's difficulties when starting school and how admission arrangements might affect them. Their study revealed that the January intake of children demonstrated more difficulties than those admitted in September. The most noticeable difficulties were those with activities requiring co-operation, persistence and language skills, such as following instructions and 'verbalising'. This study supported findings from earlier work and also confirmed that a significant number of children experiencing difficulties continued to do so during the first year in school.[4] Clearly some children will experience problems whenever they enter school. However, where they are admitted into a small discrete group with other new arrivals, the teacher is more able to focus attention on their transition needs without the additional demands of other established children.

Finally, OFSTED offer some support (albeit vague) for 4-year-olds to be in school. Their small-scale study of reception classes looked at schools with different admission policies. OFSTED found good standards of work in the majority of classes and intimated that early entry is to be recommended. Unfortunately there are no reasons given for this preference, simply an inference that more is better.[5]

These arguments for early admission to school are counterbalanced by a more recent NFER study which explored KS1 results in relation to children's birth date and their length of schooling. The results of this study indicate that children who start school close to their fourth birthday do not do as well as children born at the same time of year who start school later; this does not support the argument that the difference in achievement between autumn-born and summer-born children can be remedied by offering them the same amount of schooling.[6]

This study backs up Osborn and Millbank's research which stressed that, while preschool experience in nursery schools and playgroups had a clear beneficial effect on children's later performance, there was no data to show the benefits or detriment of early school admission.[7] However, this last finding should be treated with caution, as the research focused on the type of placement rather than the actual provision made.

In summary, there are arguments both for and against the admission of children of non-statutory age to school. The reality is that, unless there is a mass expansion of nursery education, it is probable that schools will maintain their current early admissions policies and others will seriously consider introducing it. Additionally, most parents will continue to want their children to attend school early. If we face this reality then the least we can do for young children is to consider carefully what happens to them when they come into school.

The major issue is, of course, whether 4-year-olds are receiving an education and care appropriate to their needs. This appropriate provision must recognise that children under statutory school age are strictly in the nursery age-group and ideally should qualify for a curriculum and resourcing that is developmentally appropriate. While some schools manage to approximate to this ideal, others do not. Some schools admit 4-year-olds to school on a full-time basis, and accommodate them in a room that is too small and that does not have access to an outside area. These children may be in a teaching group of thirty or more with the one teacher not trained to teach the age-group and lacking paid teaching assistants. Initially the admission of 4-year-olds to school attracted considerable attention and schools and LEAs were alerted to the need for caution. Committees of inquiry advising the government offered clear guidelines for achieving proper provision. In 1990 the report of the Committee of Inquiry chaired by Mrs Angela Rumbold recommended that 4-year-olds in reception classes should have a more generous staffing, with personnel trained for the age-group and a broad and flexible range of activities. Although LEAs received modest grants from the DES to provide inservice education and training (INSET) for the adults involved with under-5s, these were temporary and, overall, the strong and sound messages from advisory groups were not supported with necessary resources from the centre. Consequently schools are not generally well supported financially to admit children under statutory age into reception classes. Unless early admission is costed as part of formula funding from LEAs, schools have to pay for the accommodation and education of these children out of their own budgets. There are many and various interpretations of what it costs to set up an early years classroom. Even where wise and sensitive judgements are made, the money may not be there to support them. Many reception classes are run on shoestrings.

Although most children will become 5 during their time in the reception class, there is no statutory requirement for them to embark on the National Curriculum until they enter year 1. This is extremely important because it means quite clearly that the first year in school for 4-year-olds is a foundation year. Decisions will be made about curriculum breadth and balance in the light of what children already know. Before children can embark on the learning which is identified in the National Curriculum and recognisable to parents, they have to become confident in a school setting and know how to function in a classroom. Thus the reception class curriculum is a complex blend of socialisation and learning processes as well as content.

The teachers of the youngest children have often felt isolated in their work. Increasingly now, parents and governors are more aware of the significance of that first year in school as a precursor to the National Curriculum. While in some cases this awareness is matched by good knowledge of what is appropriate, this is not always the case. Too often reception class teachers continue to feel professionally alone even if their work is warmly appreciated. The first chapter in this book argues that the reception of children into school is the responsibility of all members of the school community and considers the ways in which each can contribute.

This is not a book about inspection, but it is only realistic to be clear about the current educational climate. The new inspection arrangements which require schools to have an inspection every four years includes the inspection of pupils in the reception class, whether or not they are of statutory school age. When the inspection takes place the inspection team will make judgements on the standards of achievement, quality of learning and the spiritual, moral, social and cultural development of this age-group. The team will consider the appropriateness of the quality of teaching, the arrangements for assessment, recording and reporting the children's progress to parents, the curriculum provided (including provision for equal opportunities and for those children with special educational needs), the adequacy and use of resources and accommodation, the children's welfare and the links established with parents and the community. All these aspects will be inspected for other age-groups, of course, but where a school is focusing on the reception class it is helpful to embark on a self-audit to see just how far the school's provision for, and outcomes from, its youngest children match up to the different sections of the inspection framework.

I hope that the content in the following chapters will help teachers in some aspects of their audit.

REFERENCES

1. OFSTED (1993) *First Class: The Standards and Quality of Education in Reception Classes.* HMSO, London.
2. Woodhead, M. (1989) School starts at five . . . or four years old? *Journal of Education Policy*, Vol. 4, no. 1, p. 2.
3. Mortimore, P., Sammons, L.S, Lewis, D. and Ecob, R. (1984) *School Matters.* Open Books, Wells.
4. Hughes, M., Pinkerton, G. and Plewis, I. (1979) Children's difficulties on starting infant school, *Journal of Child Psychology and Psychiatry,* Vol. 20, no. 3, pp. 187–9.
5. OFSTED (1993) *op. cit.* (note 1).
6. Sharp, C., Hutchinson, D. and Whetton, C. (1994) How do season of birth and length of schooling affect children's attainment at key stage 1? *Educational Research*, Vol. 36, no. 2, Summer, pp. 107–19.
7. Osborn, A.F. and Millbank, J.E. (1989) *The Effects of Early Education.* Clarendon Press, Oxford.

1
A JOINT ENTERPRISE

High-quality provision for young children will only be properly secured if all sections of the school community are committed to the principle and related practices, and are clear about their roles and responsibilities in helping to achieve it. This is not meant as a glib statement but is written in full recognition of the hard work involved in gaining a consensus and in encouraging all parties practically to play their part. This chapter looks at the role of each group in turn.

PARENTS

It is oversimplistic to say that the child is the sum total of his or her upbringing, as genetic endowment still plays some part in individual make-up. However, the child's personal experience prior to coming to school, including the ways in which he or she has been regarded as a person and the models of adult behaviour to which the child has been exposed will be a powerful influence on his or her attitudes to living and learning as one of a group. The strong ties with kith and kin do not lessen when the child starts school and the bulk of the child's life continues to be at home. Parents, not teachers, are primarily legally responsible for the education of their children. What then is the parents' position when their children start school? For our purposes a parent is defined as the person who has the prime responsibility, care and control for the child, and who provides the link between home and school.

For many years early years teachers have had regular contacts with parents. However, the nature and effect of those contacts have differed greatly and depended essentially on the beliefs and commitments of individual teachers and headteachers. More recently parents have become a force to be fully acknowledged. Within the last 12 years, five education Acts have established that the school is accountable to parents.

The present government's Citizen's Charter and the move towards consumerism and market forces stress the view of parents as the customers of an education service who have certain legal rights. These include

- expressing a preference of school for their children where this is practicable;
- receiving information from the school, including the results of assessments of existing children in the school;
- contributing to the management of the school as elected governors;
- attending an annual governors' meeting for parents and the right to pass resolutions;
- contributing views through the governors on the provision of sex education at the school;
- receiving an annual written report on the progress made by their children and discussing this report with a named teacher at the school;
- involvement, where applicable, in the assessment and review of children with special educational needs;
- contributing their views of the school to an inspection team; and
- receiving a summary of the inspection report and the governor's action plan to develop the school.[1]

Despite considerable advertisement from central government, many parents (and, in particular, new parents) remain largely unaware of and indeed largely uninterested in securing a number of these rights. However the responses received at parents' meetings arising from recent OFSTED inspection reflect that parents are very anxious to receive information from the school in relation to their child's programme of work and his or her progress and development. Most parents are also keen to know just how they can help their child at home, although some are tentative and reluctant to become involved for fear of doing the wrong thing. In summary, parents are less concerned with exercising their rights and powers in regard to the school than becoming well informed about, and playing their part in, what is going on. Practices which enable this to happen will be explored in later chapters.

Notwithstanding the range of contacts that schools have made with the home, historically, teachers have often underestimated just how much children learn from their parents.[2,3] Parents also are at least very modest about their influence and in some cases they are quite unaware of the central role they have in regard to their children. Brawn makes the important point that, whatever the effects of this influence – whether for good or ill – it is the most powerful force in shaping a child in the early years.[4] Schools clearly ignore this at their peril. Indeed, in recent years there has been a dramatic shift in understanding and increase in work with parents. Although Tizard *et al.* suggest that parents continue to underestimate their role and attribute their child's success at school to the school, reception teachers increasingly recognise the home influence.[5] In the best instances, studies suggest that parental involvement improved children's performance, led to higher teacher expectations, increased children's motivation and increased parents' confidence and aims for their children.[6]

However, this effective work is not always easy. It requires commitment and a good level of confidence on the part of all involved. While all parents want the best for their children, they may be differently resourced to support their aspirations. Some parents, because of their circumstances, may not feel confident working on an equal basis with the school. Brawn suggests that this is most likely where parents meet a set of criteria in relation to social disadvantage (e.g. single parent, low income, poor housing). In addition many other parents may for various reasons feel that they are disempowered when working with teachers. This places a real responsibility on staff to build initial relationships based on sensitive understandings of the parents' perceptions, and to value all that they do for their children.[7]

While parents continue to play an important role throughout their child's school career, the argument for close involvement during the first year is particularly persuasive. The younger the child the more inextricably he or she is bound to his or her family. The adjustment to school is a major move for all children: for many it is unlikely to be undertaken successfully unless there is support from home. The parents' role in relation to the first year in school will be stressed throughout this book. What remains clear is the variety of practices in operation between and even within schools. Where there are whole-school policies on home–school links, this helps a shared understanding of what the school aims to achieve. These policies are even more valuable where parents have been fully consulted and contributed to the document.

A more contentious issue is that of a home/school agreement. The notion of a home/school contract has been debated for some years. In 1988 the National Association of Headteachers (NAHT) published a discussion paper which defined and described such a document. The aim was to

- set out the expectations which schools and parents would have of each other; and
- require schools and parents to commit themselves to obligations and responsibilities implied by these expectations.[8]

The contractual element of such a document is unlikely to promote harmonious relationships. Indeed, one could argue that the very formality could kill the essence of a trusting and flexible partnership with parents. A more recent project has broadened the concept. The NAHT has worked with the Royal Society of Arts (RSA) on a 'Home/School Contracts of Partnership Project'. This has aimed to 'identify ways of establishing more open and equal relationships between school and the home, recognising both shared goals and complementary roles for teachers and parents'. This interesting venture aims to identify good practice and see how far these are replicable within the European Community.[9]

Given the sensitivities of establishing an agreement between teachers and parents, it has the benefits of clarifying respective roles and responsibilities. Sheila Wolfendale suggests that the idea of a signed understanding would 'signal commitment, reinforce the idea that "involvement" is a two-way process . . . and that rights and responsibilities are different sides of one coin, and ultimately should be a guarantee of children's best interests'.[10]

However, suggested prerequisites for a successful agreement are

- the establishment of sound reciprocal relationships between all parties involved: this implies considerable ground work between teachers and parents prior to the child starting school;
- the parents' expressed confidence that the school will provide appropriately for the child: this means ensuring that parents have access to sufficient information about the school in order to make this judgement;
- structures, policies and resources (particularly time) which enable the parent and teacher to translate the agreement into practical work with the child; and
- recognition that parents, whilst agreeing in principle to the agreement, will be differently resourced to support it: where parents are practically

prevented from attending meetings and helping in the school, then other, informal links should be developed.

In Appendix 1, one model of a home/school agreement is described which might be included as part of an induction year Brochure.

PRESCHOOL PROVIDERS

The child's first move from home could be into one of a range of settings. These provisions are explored further in the following chapter, but they have their distinct purpose and functions and are financed, staffed and organised differently. Whatever the setting, it offers a bridge for each child between home and school. Rouse and Griffin, in looking at the care and education of children under 3 years, highlight two important issues: 'children's needs for relationships with significant, responsive adults; children's needs for developmentally appropriate learning experiences.[11] The authors rightly stress that young children have the right to quality care and education in whichever provision their parents select for them.

If these issues are regarded seriously, they have major implications for both the personal and professional qualifications of the adults responsible. These adults take a lead from children and will be sensitive and responsive to their needs. Although adults with both reticent and ebullient personalities may successfully relate to very young children, a warmth and sense of humour will result in an engagement with the child. Above all, the adult will demonstrate through his or her actions that the child is all important to him or her.

The second of these issues points to the need for adults to have a thorough training in child development in order for them to recognise the significance of children's behaviour and actions.

Although the Children Act empowers local authorities to provide training for all those engaged in child care, there is no requirement to do so. This is a major weakness in the statute and sadly reflects the lack of awareness of the responsibilities of the work involved. Despite this omission, many authorities are both encouraging and requiring staff in voluntary and private provision to attend some form of training, and non-professional training courses are increasingly standardised through the National Council for Vocational Qualifications. These are important moves. However, as with teacher training, an initial course is not sufficient to ensure that preschool workers remain refreshed and in touch with new knowledge about children's growth and learning. There is a major role for staff in all settings to organise themselves and urge their associations and local authorities to provide an ongoing programme of inservice training to help sustain them in their work.

GOVERNORS

Governors have a weighty responsibility in determining with the headteacher the purpose and direction of the school. All staff are appointed by the governors; policy decisions have to be ratified by the governing body, who also hold the purse strings and decide how policies are to be funded. The great strength of governors is their lay background and the range of different experiences and perceptions that they bring to their role. Naturally, however, the extent of governors' knowledge about early years issues will vary. Some governors may have difficulty in accepting that children of 4 and 5 have very specific needs which will have costing implications in terms of staffing, accommodation and material resources. Others may, in common with parents, be unclear about how young children learn during that first year in school and lack awareness of the activities and methodologies that promote learning. Most governing bodies will be well disposed towards the work of the reception class and it does not require professional expertise to recognise when young children are well established in school and eager to learn. However, where governors couple that appreciation with a growing knowledge of child development and early years curriculum, they can make their decisions which affect this age-group from a position of strength.

There is no specific requirement for the post of parent governor. The job can entail listening to and representing the views of parents and interpreting school policies to parents. In relation to early years, the parent governor has a potentially very important role. He or she may be a front-line person for new parents to approach if they have uncertainties or worries about aspects of school life. In practice this role is underplayed as most parents will initially approach the reception teacher or head. This is understandable and probably preferable, as it is most likely the professional who is able to provide the answer. However, the parent governor does have the advantage of having been the parent of a 4- or 5-year-old. This enables him or her to see many issues through the eyes of new parents: it implies that there is scope for him or her to use these perceptions in helping both the school and the parents develop useful ways of working together.

THE HEADTEACHER

The head is appointed by the governing body to lead the school and has a delegated responsibility for the quality of teaching and learning and the standards of achievement of all pupils. Some of the factors relating to headteachers which may affect the child's initial experiences in school include the head's previous professional experience: his or her educational philosophy, organisational and management style – practical details which include finance, building and school intake.

In order to make informed judgements about learning, teaching and curriculum in the reception class, the head needs to be knowledgeable about the age-group and to have clear expectations about appropriate levels of achievement. Where reception-age children are accommodated in infant and first schools which cater for an age-group of 4–7 or 4–8, it is likely that the head will have had an early years background and be fully conversant with the learning needs of the youngest children. However, in a first school with an age range of 4–9 or a primary school with an age-group of 4–11 years, it is unlikely that many headteachers have had in-depth experience of teaching all these age-groups, and is probable that many will have a teaching background with older pupils. However, a report from OFSTED stressed that this did not necessarily constrain the quality of work, given that the head was interested about early years and supported the practice.[12]

The headteacher's educational beliefs will reflect the ways in which reception teachers feel morally supported, the status and priority accorded to the transition to school and the ways in which the governors and the rest of the staff view the provision for the youngest children. If the headteacher is convinced of the significance of the preschool years as a time for rapid learning; if he or she believes in a developmental approach to learning and is aware of the need for a sound start to schooling, then the adults working with these children will feel well supported. They will be encouraged to develop preschool links, to foster a sensitive and phased transition to school and to devise a curriculum that is matched to the child's needs and which builds on his or her previous experience.

The moral support from the headteacher and the rest of the school will help to boost the self-esteem of adults working with the youngest children. However, the beliefs also need to be translated into practical help. Practitioners themselves place the highest priority on obtaining an appropriate ratio of adults to work with this age-group. Cleave and Brown suggest that an appropriate ratio is one that allows adults to interact with the children and be involved with their activities, observing them as individuals and intervening at the right moment to extend their learning.[13] As early years teachers know, this is not always easy to achieve even given a small group of children. However, undoubtedly, the chances of success are heightened. The staffing ratio of teachers and teaching assistants for reception classes varies enormously. Formula funding has allowed some limited discretion to buy in additional staffing, but in some smaller schools where this is not possible, the additional non-teaching hours given to a reception class may mean depriving older children of this support. This strengthens the argument for having whole-school understanding and agreement about meeting the needs of the youngest age-group.

Schools vary considerably in the resources they have and the demands they have to meet from parents and children. Where the locality is economically disadvantaged, the school accommodation is generally poor and the material resources impoverished for all age-groups, then the headteacher and governors must establish priorities. A clearly defined, realistic, targeted and costed school development plan will support these priorities. Although there may be temptation to spread money thinly across the school, by focusing on one age-group at a time beginning with the reception class, the children accrue benefits as they move through the school.

TEACHERS

While the staffing ratio for the reception class is determined by the headteacher and governors, the quality of the children's learning will be heavily influenced by the attitude, commitment and expertise of the adults in the classroom. The reception teacher's task is that of an expert: the child's subsequent success in school is heavily dependent on the experience he or she offers the child in that first year.

In most schools the reception post is recognised as specialised. Many teachers are rightly wary of opting for the job, although they may be experienced and confident in teaching other infant age-groups. Too often, however, the esteem for reception teachers has centred on the physical and emotional demands of the work. Only more recently is there a growing awareness of the intellectual rigour required. Trained and experienced reception teachers have always known about the dynamic nature of their work and have traditionally been among the most enthusiastic of staff attending inservice courses. However, for some years opportunities in initial and inservice courses do not appear to have met the demand. In 1987 an HMI survey revealed that six out of every ten newly qualified teachers interviewed felt they were not adequately equipped for teaching such young children.[14] In 1988 there was evidence of unequal support for teachers of younger children.[15] The interviewees in Cleave and Brown's study believed that many reception class teachers were not sufficiently qualified or experienced in the needs of 4-year-olds.[16] Three years later, the HMI report implicitly supports this when stating that fewer than half of the teachers in the survey fully exploited the educational value of play. Certainly, high standards of achievement were clearly linked with well qualified teachers and teaching assistants.[17]

The role of the reception teacher is complex. It demands particular insights and skills which are not required of the teacher of older children. These include

- the reception into school of children from diverse backgrounds who have not shared common past experiences and whose developmental age may range from 2 to 8 years;
- assisting these individual children to become pupils and to learn as one of a group;
- recognising the whole fund of experience that each child brings to school and taking the child on in his or her learning from that point;
- providing an appropriate curriculum based on talk and first-hand activity for children who are still predominantly egocentric and who have limited concentration spans;
- planning the programme to allow for flexible groupings, for child-initiated and teacher-directed activity;
- assessing, recording and sharing with parents the progress and development of children whose learning is often private and intangible;
- explaining the early years curriculum to parents and governors who may be more conversant with a subject-focused, exam-orientated curriculum; and
- confirming the parents' central educational role and working with them to promote the child's best chances of success.

In addition, the reception teacher is a team leader. He or she is responsible for the deployment of voluntary and paid teaching assistants. He or she must ensure that they are well briefed and prepared, able to tackle their respective jobs and that they receive all the necessary feedback to get satisfaction from that work. Unless the teacher takes this responsibility for the team, the nursery is unlikely to reap the full benefit from the shared expertise and energies of these adults. Certain management and interpersonal skills are necessary for the team leader, whatever the size of the team.

THE TEACHING ASSISTANT

The curriculum and methodology required for successful work with 4-year-olds involves the teacher working for a great deal of the time with children individually or in small groups. This can only happen when there is another adult working with the rest of the group. Although traditionally in nursery classes the assistant is a qualified nursery nurse, this has been less evident in mainstream classes. HMI reported in 1992 that often classroom assistants have little training and most are dependent on the teacher for guidance on their work. Although in the majority of cases assistants were observed to be well briefed and supervised, their roles were demanding and diffuse. In some cases the teacher's planning did not sufficiently clearly identify the work of the assistant.[18]

In this survey HMI observed teaching assistants playing a particularly valuable role in

- supporting children during the initial transition into school;
- enabling children to have access to a range of curriculum activities, which would not be possible given the attention of only one adult;
- giving attention to those children who have difficulties in adjusting to school; and
- releasing the teacher to spend time with those children who are at the early stages of beginning to read and write.

However, HMI also make the general point that 'perhaps the greatest constraint on their effectiveness was a limited perception on the part of schools, and of non-teaching staff themselves, of the extent to which they could provide support'.[19]

Where a qualified nursery nurse is employed it is perhaps easier immediately to adopt the nurse as a co-partner in the classroom. Although the training for a nursery nurse is shorter and more practically orientated than for teacher training, the nursery nurse is, nevertheless, qualified to work alongside the teacher, helping to plan, promote, assess and record children's learning. With an untrained teaching assistant these aspects of work must be learnt, both through some organised training and through working alongside the teacher. Since the HMI survey there has been increased awareness of the value of trained teaching assistants, particularly in reception classes. Inservice courses for teaching assistants are rapidly increasing and a number of LEAs are using targeted inservice monies for this purpose. In addition, the government proposes funding accredited courses. The successful completion of course and related classroom experience could contribute towards accreditation of a BEd qualification for qualified teacher status.[20]

School-based training varies, but is arguably most valuable, being tailor-made for the role. Sometimes preparation for the job is carefully staged. HMI describe good practice in one school where the prerequisite for a paid non-teaching post is to have worked for a period as a voluntary helper in the school. The headteacher introduces each voluntary helper to the work involved and assigns each one to a teacher. The volunteers work under the close supervision of the teacher. They also receive regular training from the headteacher, who explains school policies and practices and encourages discussion. The head and teachers constantly monitor the work of the volunteers in order to get to know their interests, strengths and skills. Vacancies for mid-day supervisory assistants and teaching assistants are filled by voluntary helpers, whose capabilities are already known. HMI observed that the commitment and time given to preparing and supporting all paid and voluntary assistants in the school resulted in enhanced job satisfaction for the adults and improved learning opportunities for the children.[21]

Despite this, the need for induction and ongoing support for teaching assistants is variable and in some schools still non-existent. Although there is general appreciation for their work, their status and financial remuneration is low. HMI report that too often they had no job description, no formal or informal appraisal of performance and insufficient time to do the job.[22] These requirements must be met in order to shift the thinking from the teaching assistant being simply an 'extra pair of hands' to a full member of the professional team.

VOLUNTARY ASSISTANTS

Parents and members of the community can play a valuable part as volunteer helpers in a reception class. Essentially by their presence they will help to increase the staffing ratio. By inviting parents into school, teachers are offering them insights into what happens during the school day. In the reception class this is particularly valuable when the nature of learning is not always clear to the lay person. In addition, in any community there is a great deal of energy, talent and expertise to be harnessed. The resourceful school will particularly identify those people who can relate to young children and who are prepared to offer their skills in the classroom.

The nature of involvement can vary from an occasional contribution to play an instrument or help with an outing to a regular commitment to help in the classroom. In the latter case the regular aspect of the work needs to be stressed. The teacher who finds that his or her carefully planned lesson has to be abandoned at the last minute due to the unexplained absence of a voluntary assistant quickly learns not to depend on this support and consequently does not delegate any substantial responsibilities to the assistant. Inevitably the voluntary nature of the work means that there is no contractual commitment. However, most responsible volunteers will accept the need to be reliable.

Where the commitment is regular, the volunteer has an entitlement to be inducted into the work and to see how his or her role fits into the totality of the classroom planning. An induction for voluntary assistants should include sensitive reference to a code of conduct. Whether or not there is a written code of conduct for all staff, there will be implicit understandings about the need for confidentiality in relation to information received about pupils' behaviour and work in school. Increasingly a whole-school behaviour policy will include guidelines on appropriate conduct for both adults and children. When working in school, volunteers should be accepted as full team members and accorded the courtesies that go with this role. In return they should be prepared to agree to the rulings which guide their relationships with others.

REFERENCES

1. Department for Education (DfE) (1992) *Education (Schools) Act.* HMSO, London.
2. Tizard, B. and Hughes, M. (1984) *Young Children Learning*. Fontana, London.
3. Mayall, B. (1990) Childcare and childhood, *Children and Society*, Vol. 4, no. 4.

4. Brawn, D. (1992) Working with parents, in G. Pugh (ed.) *Contemporary Issues in the Early Years.* Paul Chapman Publishing/National Children's Bureau, London.
5. Tizard, B., Blatchford, P., Burke, J., Clare, F. and Plewis, I. (1988) *Young Children at School in the Inner City.* Lawrence Erlbaum Associates, Hove and London.
6. Woodhead, M. (1985) *Intervening in Disadvantage.* NFER/Nelson, Slough.
7. Brawn (1992) *op. cit.* (note 4).
8. National Association of Headteachers (1988) *Home/School Contract of Partnership: A Discussion Paper.* NAHT, Haywards Heath.
9. Jones, G., Bastiani, J., Bell, G. and Chapman, C. (1992) *A Willing Partnership.* Royal Society of Arts, London.
10. Wolfendale, S. (1992) *Empowering Parents and Teachers: Working for Children.* Cassell, London, p. 114.
11. Rouse, D. and Griffin, S. (1992) Quality for the under threes, in G. Pugh (ed.) *Contemporary Issues in the Early Years.* Paul Chapman Publishing, London, p. 142.
12. OFSTED (1993) *First Class: The Standards and Quality of Education in Reception Classes.* HMSO, London.
13. Cleave. S. and Brown, S. (1991) *Early to School: Four Year Olds in Infant Classes.* NFER/Nelson, Slough.
14. DES (1987) *The New Teacher in School.* HMSO, London.
15. Sharp, C. (1988) Starting school at four: research findings and implications. Paper presented at the NFER Conference, 'Starting school at four: planning for the future', Solihull Conference Centre.
16. Cleave and Brown (1991) *op. cit.* (note 13).
17. OFSTED, (1993) *op. cit.* (note 12).
18. Her Majesty's Inspectors of Schools (HMI) (1992) *Education Observed: Non-Teaching Staff in Schools.* HMSO, London.
19. *Ibid.,* p. 14.
20. Department for Education (1993) *The Initial Training of Primary School Teachers: New Criteria for Courses* (Circular 14/93, paras 32–3). HMSO, London.
21. HMI (1992) *op. cit.* (note 18).
22. *Ibid.*

2

THE INTRODUCTION TO SCHOOL

Starting school is a momentous event for each child and consequently for each parent, particularly if it is a first or only child. The ways in which schools help children settle into their first class can profoundly affect patterns of learning and behaviour for the future.

SELECTING A SCHOOL

In the past parents were expected to send their child to the school in their locality and firm rules were applied about catchment areas for schools. In theory now, at least, there is opportunity for a choice of establishment. Some parents increasingly respond to encouragement from the government and the media to scrutinise establishments and to examine critically the provision offered. Sometimes, though, parents' criteria for judging a school is based on limited knowledge of what an early years establishment should offer. However, a recent study in which a large sample of parents were interviewed about their reasons for choosing a school for their children reflects a strong common view. The majority of parents regard locality as of prime importance, although a significant number did pay regard to the reputation of the school. The report indicates that, in general, parents do not exercise a wide choice when deciding on their child's school, although the study also revealed that most parents would consider moving their child from school if he or she was clearly unhappy. When questioned about the characteristics of a good school, this group of parents regarded good relationships among parents, teachers and children, the aptitude and attitudes of staff, a positive ethos and good discipline as all important. By comparison, the physical resources of the school and academic results are not so highly regarded.[1]

It is important that headteachers recognise the factors which influence parents in making their choice about a school for their child. It is also necessary to accept that it is unlikely that a school will meet with the requirements of all parents. A school operates from a position of strength if it makes clear to parents its aims and purposes, and secures the allegiance of the parents who are prepared to support those aims. This makes it possible to capitalise on the tremendous enthusiasm, interest and energy shown by most new parents when their child starts school. This is the ideal; I also acknowledge that in some areas parents have little awareness of their opportunity for choice and, even if they do, they lack the time, energy or finance for transport to exercise it. These parents will opt for the local school automatically but, in doing so, may not be aware of the very significant role they might play in offering support. In these circumstances the school has the task of helping parents to recognise their central place in the development of their child. This can be daunting work, but if successful does mean that the school's work is strengthened, the child receives his or her entitlement from home and the parents are empowered in the knowledge and pleasure of being effective in their child's learning and development.

POTENTIAL EARLY DISCONTINUITIES

Prior to coming to school young children will have had a range of different experiences. These experiences will profoundly affect the way they view school and the adjustments they make.

Home experiences will vary. Most children will have already spent time away from home, with childminders, in a nursery or a playgroup. Only a small number of children will come to school direct from home. Within this group it is important to distinguish the families that opt for their own good reasons not to send their children to a preschool setting as opposed to those whose circumstances prevent it. For instance, the latter group may include children from 'homeless' families in temporary accommodation who may have missed out on preschooling and also be sharing the stress experienced by the family as a result of their homelessness.

The children's home backgrounds will, of course, be different. After interviewing parents about their children's preschool circumstances, Barratt suggests that housing, the financial situation and the social life of the family were influential, together with the opportunities that parents provided for playing and learning.[2] Social class is not seen as a strong divisive factor: most homes offer toys and opportunities for talk with their children. However, one study found that middle-class parents tend to opt for more specifically educational toys and books and encouraged their children more directly towards early literacy and numeracy.[3] The strong message is that families in general offer a very special context for young children learning. Dunn emphasises how even children as young as 2 years can respond to emotions within their family and can understand the expectations that govern behaviour within a household.[4] Other studies stress how parents can support early literacy and numeracy development in the home by working closely with the school (see Chapters 4 and 6). Raven's study refers to some of these home/school learning programmes, but it goes further and claims that some families create better conditions for their preschool children learning than any school setting. Raven suggests that they do this, not because they formally prepare the children for schooling, but because they use sensitive ways of nurturing important qualities of motivation and aspects of competence, which include the ability to think, project ahead, communicate and appraise what they are doing. These parents later support their children in school, not by copying what the school does but by giving children confidence and the ability to think for themselves. Raven explains that many families do not achieve this, because they have different value systems where the qualities and competencies described are not seen as important; also, economic and environmental reasons prevent some parents from having the personal energy and confidence to treat their children in this developmental manner.[5] These findings serve to emphasise the enormous educational potential of parents as well as the range of different starting points that young children will have on admission to school.

While childminders will offer young children some experiences akin to home, those who have attended playgroups and nurseries will be familiarised with some aspects of institutional life. However, it should not be assumed that where this has happened a child will necessarily find a move to school any easier. There has been no recent research on continuity from preschool to school, and the major data is still from the NFER study undertaken between 1977 and 1980. This will be referred to in some detail as it is significant that some 15 years later many messages remain valid. The study suggests that, whatever the previous experience, on arrival at school children are likely to encounter discontinuities associated with the setting, the curriculum and the people.[6]

The buildings which house preschool settings will range from private houses and large halls to purpose-built units. On moving to primary school, children will experience the greatest changes where the scale, size and complexity of building is different; where facilities such as lavatories and playgrounds are located differently and where there are organisational restrictions on the children's movements, particularly within classrooms.

Looking at curriculum in the broadest sense, there are potential sources of discontinuity for children in regard to the type and availability of the content and the daily routines. While playgroups and nurseries may provide some similar activities, the range of provision is likely to be greater in a purpose-built nursery, together with opportunities for maintaining and extending permanent areas for specific experiences. A designated reception class may offer a similar learning environment to a nursery. However, where a mixed age-group is accommodated, the activities available for the youngest children must necessarily be limited to part of the classroom.

One notable difference may be in the equipment used to promote gross physical development and the provision for outdoor play. The PE apparatus used mainly in the hall will replace the wheeled toys which are available in most preschool settings. Access to outside play may not have been possible for many children attending playgroup, but for those in nursery schools and classes access may have been freely available throughout the sessions. In school all children will have access to the outside at set times, and some reception classes may have their own identified outside area. However, the range and quality of equipment outside can vary from an area richly resourced for physical, imaginative and investigative play, to a sterile patch of space.

One of the greatest changes for new children is the opportunity for involvement in the curriculum. While some preschool settings offer limited opportunities for choice, the majority of nurseries and playgroups enable children to have unlimited access to different activities for a substantial part of the programme, with adults supporting or becoming involved with small groups. In reception classes the most prevalent mode is for children to be engaged in prescribed activities while the teacher targets his or her time with different groups in turn. The transition into school usually means a restriction of choice for many children.

Most children from different preschool settings will not be familiar with many of the daily routines which are part of school life. Most vulnerable times are the daily transitions: moving into the hall, being in the playground, changing for PE and lunchtimes. The notion of a formal playtime is particularly alien, as the majority of children will not have experienced being required to set aside an activity in order to go outside for a set period of time. Stephenson refers to the nonsense of interrupting children's play 'to go out to play' as a feature of traditional organisation found in some reception classes.[7]

When starting school a child may move into a setting with larger numbers of children. It may be that the class group size will not be so large as that experienced in a large playgroup or nursery class. However, as Cleave, Jowett and Bate point out, the fluctuations in the size of group experienced throughout the school day may be considerable. The study describes one new child who had settled into her class group, but who reacted with confusion and distress when she experienced, typically during the course of one morning, the following group sizes:

Assembly (whole school)	360
Classroom activities	31
Playtime (infants only)	170
Special prereading group	9
Television with another class	60
Dinner (first sitting)	110

The ways in which children spend their time also differs from preschool to school settings. In the same study, in playgroups and nurseries children spent more time mixing with their peers than in infant classes. Once in school they were involved in more whole-class compulsory activities, during which the child participated alongside others but without any collaboration. Typical examples included watching television, listening to the teacher and pencil-and-paper activity.[8]

Until recently the ratio of adults to children in all preschool settings will have been more favourable as compared to that in infant classes. Where there have been moves to have teaching assistants working alongside the teacher, this has clearly reduced the differential. However, the amount and quality of adult time that young children have had at preschool is not always directly related to the ratio of adults available. Thomas observed a small group of children in a nursery for a day and managed to record every utterance from them and from the adults. She found that teachers were prepared to accept minimal comments from children and that their own exchanges with the children rarely helped to develop discourse or thinking skills.[9] In the Oxford Pre-school Research Study, Woods reports that 'incidence of really interesting talk is rare'.[10] This study and others in the 1980s [11,12] have helped to raise teacher awareness of their role in developing talk from the earliest age. My own, more recent observations in nursery classes reflect a variable picture but one in which many staff use their time to converse with children. Moreover, although these studies indicated that the adults did not always use their time to interact most profitably with children, they are available to the children. In a flexible nursery or playgroup setting, a child is able to approach an adult with an ease which is not always possible in a reception class when the teacher and teaching assistant are focusing their time with particular groups of children.

Some of the major changes that children face on admission will be examined later in more detail. The important point here is that the very wide range of experiences that a child may have had accentuates the gap between those best prepared and those least prepared for starting school.

SHARED ROLES AND RESPONSIBILITIES

The main developments since 1982 when Cleave, Jowett and Bate reported major gaps in contacts among teachers, preschool staff and parents have been directed towards helping all parties to become more informed about what each provides for the child. Regular practices now include exchange visits among home, school, playgroups and nurseries, and a range of informative literature produced by nurseries and schools for parents. Many schools with limited resources give a considerable amount of time and energy to forging these preschool links and, because of this, it is important that outcomes are clearly targeted. These should include opportunities

- for all parents to become more aware of the educational value of life in the home;
- to understand the significance of the playgroup, nursery and reception curriculums and how each contributes to their child's subsequent well-being and achievement;
- for preschool staffs to become familiar with the curriculum and organisation offered and the expectations of children in reception classes;

- to identify sources of match and mismatch with their own provisions;
- for teachers to gain as full a picture as possible of each child's past experiences, interests and achievements prior to starting school;
- to recognise respect and support the vital role that parents and carers play in their child's progress and development; and
- for all parties to recognise the value of working in harmony to support the child.

This is an ambitious programme and requires a range of approaches which are rigorously evaluated in order to ensure that they are meeting the needs of all parties involved.

INITIAL CONTACT WITH THE FAMILY

The period of time that elapses between the parents registering their child and the point of admission to school offers rich opportunities for all parties to exchange information. For parents, the question is always about how their child will adapt to the first step in his or her school career. The Education Acts (1988 and 1992) include explicit and compulsory requirements for parents to have access to certain information.[13] However, no legislation is likely to identify the issues that concern parents most sharply. These may include the worry of how their child will adapt to a new regime and environment, what will be expected of him or her and how he or she will relate to other children. These issues will inevitably precede any concerns about the curriculum and yet curriculum content is often the central part of the school brochure.

Clear and comprehensive documentation about the school is important and, of course, to some extent mandatory. An attractive and informative school brochure can also be an effective means of advertising the school. Sometimes, however, in the desire to include everything, a school brochure can end up a general repository. The NFER study reported that, typically, the topics included induction arrangements, curriculum, health and safety arrangements, class and staffing details, arrangements for parental involvement, daily school procedures and details of extra-curricular activities. Nearly all the schools in this study offered information for parents on how to teach letter formation to their children.[14]

There is, of course, some merit in keeping all information together.

However, there is also a danger of information overload for parents. Perhaps there is a case for a brochure which focuses on the induction year and which provides all the information for that year.

Written information is helpful for parents but however well presented, it is not a sufficient means of communication. The initial visit to the school is important in offering personal contacts as well as providing the opportunity to see the school in action. Because this visit is so important it needs careful planning and time allocated to it. For this reason when parents call in unannounced on their first visit, it is preferable to limit this meeting to a brief, friendly discussion and arrange for a further visit at a mutually convenient time.

Families will have gained considerable information about school life prior to their visit. This information is not always helpful. Neighbours and friends may have given conflicting messages. The planned initial visit to the school importantly gives the parents and child a first-hand impression of school life. For the oldest child in a family who has not attended a nursery class or school, this is likely to be his or her first experience of a school building. The parents' last experiences may have been during their own school days. Both parents and child will have misgivings, anxieties, hopes and expectations in regard to starting school. Some of these may be framed in questions but others may be hazy and unfocused. The visit should aim for the parents to share their views of education, to talk about their expectations for their child when he or she starts school and to receive information which will help them to decide whether this school is the place in which these expectations can be fulfilled. Sometimes parents find it difficult to gather that information or even understand exactly what is happening in terms of teaching and learning. My own observations of parents being given a tour of the school and being taken into busy classrooms, which are staffed by a range of adults, are evidence of this. Talking to parents afterwards, they admit to remembering little of the building layout, and to have insufficient time for questions. Above all they were confused about the roles of different adults in classrooms and the purposes of classroom activity. 'Do all those people teach the kids and is that what happens all day? [with reference to a range of play activities linked to literacy and maths development]. I think that my boy will be ready for a bit more when he starts.' However, other parents were hugely appreciative of headteachers giving time to answer their queries and making very real efforts to explain how the school functions.

The head will also have his or her own agenda of information to gather. By providing a welcoming atmosphere and a genuine interest in the family, the head can encourage parents to talk openly and freely about their child and so gain a number of insights into the child's lifestyle, experiences, interests and abilities. The head will want to present the school to the family and to stress the importance of and opportunities for working in partnership with parents. Importantly, however, the head should explain that it is not mandatory for children to come to school until they are of statutory school age. Parents do need to be encouraged to exercise choice in this matter. Many parents are not aware that choice is an option: even if they are aware, the advent of the National Curriculum means that others are concerned that their children's chances of success at 7 years might be at risk if they do not enter school early. Headteachers have the sensitive task of explaining to parents that, whilst for young 4-years-olds admitted to school in September an additional year of appropriate education should offer a good foundation for statutory education, it is oversimplistic to assume that there will automatically be significant gains in learning.

Above all, these first visits give strong impressions to parents and children about the sort of place that school is. The initial reception they receive, the time allocated and interest shown towards the needs of the family and the approachability of the staff will set the tone for future contacts.

FAMILIARISATION WITH THE SCHOOL

New parents and children need time and opportunities to become acquainted with the school accommodation and what happens inside it. If at all possible the aim should be to ensure that, when the child finally starts school, both the child and his or her parents feel reasonably secure with the building and routines and both teacher and teaching assistant are known persons to approach. If this is to be achieved it will involve a series of visits, meetings and contacts.

After all these years, home visiting remains a contentious issue. Where a school is committed to home visiting, the head and staff will somehow find the time to organise it. Schools in very different locations support home visits, but the strongest argument for them must be in those areas where parents do not readily approach the school. When making the decision about whether to use valuable teacher time for home visits, the school will want carefully to evaluate the resulting gains. These are most often related to the benefits of securing a sound parent–teacher relationship. Establishing an initial social link with the child is also appreciated, as well as the opportunity for the teacher to find out important information about the child within the home setting. What seems to be underemphasised is the child's reaction to a home visit. Cousins asked some 4-year-olds for their reactions to the initial visit received by their teacher, and the very strong message was that all the children valued highly the opportunity for this personal link. They perceived the teacher as coming to meet them, to see their toys and share their interests. Where this did not happen because the teacher was more involved in admission forms, the child was sadly disappointed.[15]

The aim of familiarising children with school prior to entry is to ensure that the trauma of the transition is minimised. When children are able to become acquainted, at first as spectators with aspects of school life, they are able to take stock and observe conventions and routines without feeling pressurised into taking part in activities. Opportunities to do this will help children move forward in confidence towards becoming participants. In order for parents to support the school and to recognise their central educational role, they need to gain a detailed picture of school life, understand just how best they can help their child at home and how they can work in close liaison with the teacher.

The ways in which schools plan for and organise this process of familiarisation will depend on their resources, their geographical location and the needs of their families.

ADMISSION POLICIES AND PRACTICES

Although preadmission procedures should help to ensure that young entrants look forward to starting school, the reality of starting is different. Children recognise that this time it is 'for real' in the build up to the big day at home, and by participating in such rituals as dressing in new clothes and packing a school bag. In most families the first day at school for a child is recognised as an important occasion, and the adults in school can help to participate in this 'rite of passage' by showing that they acknowledge the mixed emotions experienced by parents and child on the day. However well the school has worked with families prior to school, the event of the first day will still give rise to some discontinuities. This is inevitable and most young children are able not only to cope with a degree of difference but will also find it stimulating.

The expectation from all concerned will be that school offers something new and, occasionally, there is a sense of disappointment when the child feels that he or she is getting only more of the same already experienced at playgroup or nursery. Despite this, Cleave, Jowett and Bate stress that it is important that the degree of change is not sufficient to 'shock'.[16] This depends on planning a sensitive admission.

The organisation of the reception into school still varies considerably. The NFER study on admissions policies revealed that the majority of schools having 4-year-olds admitted them on a full-time basis.[17] Many parents would support this as a natural progression from the part-time attendance experienced at playgroup or nursery. However, this view neglects to realise the stress involved in making another transition and being a novice once more. Most children of reception age and in particular the young 4-year-olds will find five full days a week initially overwhelming, and will benefit from part-time placement at least during the first few weeks.

The size of school is an important factor for young children. Small schools admit a smaller number of children and so find it easier to make the transition to school informal and focused on the individual. In larger schools a phased entry can allow each child in turn initially to have more adult time and attention.

The ideal should be to offer the family a first day in school that is tailored to their needs. Time spent in this way on day one may well avoid problems and anxieties arising at a later date. This does mean allowing additional time for such rituals as finding pegs and hanging up coats, for listening to parents and child, and time to ensure that they are all comfortable with procedures. There are considerable benefits therefore of dealing with only small groups of newcomers and thus having a staggered admission to school, with each group of children admitted over a period of time. This can take as long as the school feels is acceptable, but usually occurs over a period of up to half a term. The crucial factor is that each new group initially has time and attention from adults in school to help initiate it into the classroom routines and expectations.

An initial degree of flexibility in starting and finishing times of sessions can also help children to receive a more individual daily welcome to school, offer opportunities for exchange of information with parents and reducing an institutionalised beginning and end to the school day. These are the undoubted benefits. Teachers will also recognise the potential disruption of families drifting into the class at all times, of not being able to have a coherent start to the day with all children and of the overall times of sessions being reduced. This must be a matter of negotiation between schools and parents. The important question behind the decisions made, however, must be in relation to the welfare and progress of both the individual child and the class as a whole.

The overall desirability for parents initially to spend some time in school with their children is well recognised. However, once again the rules need to accommodate individual needs. Consideration of the child's past experience in being separated from home and observations of his or her levels of confidence and adaptability in the school setting must play a part when deciding when it is appropriate for the parents to leave the child. The opportunity for parents to stay for a while in a parents' room in the school can offer a helpful bridge in this process.

The variations in admission procedures in schools can cause misunderstandings between families. Schools within a locality can have very different practices in relation to preparation for school, the length of the school day for newcomers and the arrangements for settling the child. Jacqui Cousins in her study describes the reactions of one parent of a reception child who became angry when required initially to stay with her child. This parent was well aware that her son's friends, starting at a nearby school, were not accompanied by parents and she saw no reason for a different practice.[18] This, of course, raises a number of issues, above all the need for the school clearly to justify its practices to parents.

Organisation of teaching groups in school will affect the nature of the reception-age children. One school of thought supports the reception children being in a mixed age-group: this, they argue, allows this youngest group to be accommodated as a smaller number and to be offered the support of a model from the older children in class. For small primary schools the organisation of age-groups is determined for them, and teachers may have their new intake within an age-group of 4–7. Where schools do have a choice, however, it is worth them considering the joint recommendations given by the British Association for Early Childhood Education and the Pre-Schools Playgroup Association who state firmly that 4-year-olds are happier with a group of their peers and younger children than with those older than themselves.[19] This points to children being accommodated in school as a discrete group. The argument for a separate reception class is echoed by teachers who were involved in a pilot exercise on early entry to infant school organised in four London boroughs. One teacher accommodating 4-year-olds in a mixed-age class described it as 'like trying to teach a class of bright, motivated and well taught children and run a creche at the same time'.[20]

Clearly a mixed age-group with its wide developmental span of needs will be more challenging for the teacher than one chronological age-group. This form of organisation is also expensive of resources in terms of materials and apparatus and also space, which is sufficient to meet active play needs and to ensure that older children have sufficient privacy for more sedentary work. The most persuasive argument, however, must be related to the age and stage of development of reception children, most particularly young 4-year-olds. These children are not yet of statutory school age and should not be required to participate in the statutory National Curriculum. The induction into school should ensure a curriculum and organisation which is centred on helping the child to make sense of school, to experience success and to extend his or her learning and social development. This can best be done in an environment which is solely given over to the needs of children at that stage of their school career.

ADJUSTING TO SCHOOL

Many parents can give first-hand accounts of their child, stating that he or she has enjoyed the first day in school but that the child has decided that he or she will not return tomorrow. Where this happens the chances are that the initial excitement and the sense of novelty have diminished and that the child senses challenges ahead for which he or she feels ill prepared. Even if this reluctance to continue with school life is not made explicit or even indicated, it is helpful if all participating adults are aware of the factors involved for a child in making a secure adjustment to school. This awareness can help both parents and assistants to make their best efforts to create a school day which will minimise the child's difficulties and alert them to a child showing signs of confusion or distress. Willes points out that, at the affective, emotional level, the child's problems are appreciated and the teachers in her study were observed making great efforts to be supportive. However, she argues that, in order really to help the child, more is required. Teachers need to be very clear about what is happening in classroom interactions and so must aim to assist the child in becoming an active and effective participant.[21]

Having looked generally at the possible discontinuities experienced by children moving from previous settings, we now look more carefully at two aspects of school life, namely, school routines and procedures and the language exchanges involved in teaching and learning.

School routines form a large part of the pattern of each child's daily experience. Because the teacher is responsible for his or her class, the routines and procedures are firmly in the teacher's control. The newcomer to school is required to understand and participate in these daily organisational matters. While some of these requirements are simply designed to promote social cohesion in the group, this is not always the case. Cook-Gumperz stresses that 'familiarity with the subtleties of classroom organisation is a pre-condition for gaining access to learning opportunities'.[22]

Teachers generally take great pains to explain to children what is required of them in school. Children may have some difficulties in complying with these requirements when they do not match with previous experiences. Where children have never been expected to clear up their toys and materials at home or at playgroup, this requirement in school is not always welcomed. However in a class environment where the reasons for doing things are clearly spelt out, and where adults work alongside children in helping them achieve tidy work habits, these problems are usually overcome. More seriously, when children are asked to do strange things like 'take off your clothes for PE' without any prior experience of this routine, most are understandably going to interpret this literally and on reaching a naked state they can become very upset when this is seen to be the wrong action to take.

Children will do their best to please their teacher even if their actions do not seem to comply with the teacher's requirements. Margaret Jackson describes what Donna did following her teacher's instructions. Donna's class was told to get out writing books, pencils and name cards, sit at a table and practise writing their names. The teacher's stated intention was for children to practise letter formation and to help them learn how to write their own names. Donna eventually found a pencil, then sharpened it and found a space in which to sit. She did not write but began comparing her name card with that of her neighbour. She counted, compared and named all the letters. After five minutes the teacher arrived and told Donna off for not getting on with her work.[23] Although Jackson intimates that Donna made sense of the activity despite having not understood the teacher's requirements, this is not clear from the incident. It is also possible that Donna may have understood the task initially, but during the time that elapsed between the teacher briefing and her settling down to work Donna may have forgotten.

Observations of reception classes show this to be a common occurrence. The task is not part of the child's agenda, which may mean that his or her motivation is not sufficiently high to place it as a priority in the child's memory. Given other distractions it is feasible that Donna is left only with a hazy recall of the task and her name card to give her some clues. She then uses her experience and knowledge of written language to find out more about words and so aims to please. However, as far as the teacher was concerned, Donna did not meet the demands of the task and was causing some disruption. Jackson points out that relevant use of past experience and knowledge are not enough in the classroom. Confirmation to expected behaviour patterns is what is also required by busy teachers.[24] If this is so then young children must be clear about teacher instructions and expectations (see Chapter 4). The need for the teacher to see school life through the eyes of the child is a common theme running through this book. The ability to do this is critical when initiating newcomers to school: without it messages delivered will be misunderstood and will result in confused and failing children.

Commonly, young children are anxious about other routines which are often part-and-parcel of institutionalised school life. In Barratt's study, reception-age children recall disliking sitting on an uncarpeted floor, being required to cross their legs (physically difficult for small children) and lining up to go into school.[25] Since this study many such formalised rituals have thankfully been abandoned and recognised as being particularly inappropriate for 4- and 5-year-olds. The fact that children are very sensitive to adult approval and will do their best to please places tremendous responsibility on the adults to ensure that school routines and rules are reasonable, necessary and supportive to children. Even where routines are quickly learnt by children, such as the practice of registration, the stress involved should not be underestimated: the child is required to sit in silence, listen to his or her name being called and avoid responding to the calling of any other names. Thought might be given to possible less formal alternatives which serve the same adult purpose.

The process of registration uses a common routine which is inevitably necessary given the responsibility of managing a group of children. It is described by Sinclair and Coulthard as 'bidding'.[26] It involves the teacher giving a cue which acts as an open invitation for children to respond to a question. It might include a direct invitation to 'put your hands up' or a request for 'who can tell me?', or more indirectly, 'I wonder what?' In each case the correct responses to the cue will be for the child to raise his or her hand, thus making a bid to speak and, when nominated, to respond knowing that he or she should not be interrupted by other children. Moreover, children who respond to a bid can expect the teacher to indicate whether the response was correct or acceptable, simply by a 'good' or 'well done'. Significantly, if the answer is incorrect or not relevant, the teacher's response will be non-committal rather than negative. Bidding is common in all classrooms and is learnt remarkably quickly by most children within the first term at school. It is a useful social and behavourial mechanism but it is not a routine that comes easily to young children. It should not, for example, be assumed that 4-year-olds are necessarily interested in what other children are saying, or if they are quiet they are actively participating.

One major requirement when adjusting to school is for children to understand the rules governing classroom discourse. Willes likens these rules to a game. She suggests that the teacher knows the game well and he or she encourages the children to play their part as fully as possible. This is clearly seen in whole-class discussions, where the teacher invites children to recall an aspect from a story recently told. Some children, knowing the rules, will play their part fully and provide a reasonable and appropriate response. Other children may fail to understand the question, may not identify the question as relevant for them or, on being directly questioned, may fail to give a relevant answer. This, Willes suggests, can be seen as a wrong or missing move and, in this case, the teacher acts to offer further clues or to play the move him or herself and to supply the right answer.[27] These rules apply to most circumstances in the classroom where the teacher directs talk. In order to feel in control, a child must know the rules of the game and use them for his or her own purposes, both to demonstrate to the teacher what the child knows and to acquire further understanding and knowledge. Mary Willes further suggests that few children question the teacher or seek for clarification. It is rare (but very refreshing) to find the type of question posed by Sonny Boy, a wonderfully gifted traveller boy who asked his teacher 'why do you keep asking the kids questions when you knows all the answers? Like . . . like . . . what colour is it then. You can see for yourself it's red . . . so why do you keep asking them?' Cousin's observations of Sonny Boy made it clear that he had not learnt the first rules of classroom discourse, to be quiet and listen until invited to speak.[28]

We have stressed the different foundational experiences for children starting school. Some will slip into the role of pupil easily, others will have great difficulty in learning what is expected. Willes points out that some of this learning can only be picked up through classroom experience. Children will come to recognise the teacher's use of language:

for instance, that when the teacher asks a question about a forbidden activity, it should be understood as an instruction to stop it; that when the teacher responds to the child's answer in a non-committal way, this should be interpreted as a negative response.[29]

In learning to adjust to the classroom, children will seek help from one another. Less confident children will listen to their more successful peers and imitate the responses which they observe have received commendation from the teacher. Willes suggests that, although this imitation is not always favoured by the teacher, it can be an important step for a child who is trying to understand what is happening and moving towards tentative participation.[30]

The child's adjustment to school is a personal matter for each family. It will depend on how both the adults in school and at home take their cues from the child and respond to early signs of stress and anxiety.

A major benefit for the individual who has successfully adjusted is for him or her to feel part of the establishment. Christine Pascal describes rites of incorporation by which the child is helped to identify with the school.[31] Parents and preschool groups will prepare the child for this school incorporation through the ways in which they introduce the notion of school and the practical steps which parents take in buying new clothes and equipment which is required as part of assuming the new role of pupil. Throughout the first year in school this new identity will be re-enforced.

Suggested action

Headteacher

- Review the school/community links that exist to enable the school to make contact with young families. These might include using shops, libraries and health centres to display the work of the school and to provide information about registration for new children.
- Visit local playgroups and mother-and-toddler clubs to offer informal talks about procedures for starting school. Check with local health visitors that all children on their lists register for school in good time.
- Create a welcoming atmosphere for parents to include a welcome sign on the school door or at the school gate; attractive signs indicating directions to the school office; a large-scale plan of the school layout and photographs of every member of the school staff

with captions describing their roles; and instructions for visitors who arrive when there is no one to receive them.

- Provide an area for families in your school. However small, this can help to set the tone for home/school relationships and it can serve a variety of purposes. These include use as a base for mother-and-toddler meetings; toy library and play-pack lending services; a workroom for parents making resources for the preschool children; for informal meetings between new and established parents and governors; a quiet interview room; and for the school doctor.

- Aim for you and your staff to gain as full a picture as possible about children's lifestyles and learning prior to coming to school: visit preschool settings and consider the match between what is offered there and at school in terms of range of curriculum content, opportunities for independence, routines and adult expectations; if possible, include childminders in home visits.

- Arrange a carefully planned first visit for families:

  - Outline a simple programme indicating what the visit will cover and giving names of the key people whom families will meet; attach a plan of the school (if this is not in the school brochure). An overall time for the visit may be helpful to parents and will help with your time management.

  - Use at least half of the time to meet privately with the family; aim to have this meeting in comfortable surroundings and provide a cup of tea. Encourage parents to talk freely and positively in their own time about their child (an extended opportunity for this is more valuable than a number of group sessions). Expect the parents to do most of the talking and ask if you may take notes. If the child is present, ensure that there are interesting activities for him or her and make a special time when the child is the focus of attention.

  - Ask parents about their expectations for their child during the first year in school and encourage them to see what role they have to play in this process. If parents and child have already decided that this is the school for them, provide them with written details and dates of the events which will take place prior to the child's admission.

- Review your admission policy and practices with a working group of governors, parents, teachers and assistants. Collect responses from prospective and new parents who have been asked what they need

Suggested Action contd.

to know in the period between registration and admission of their child to school. Use this material when considering any changes you might make.

- Review your written communications with a group of parents and consider the following:

  - Audience: do you provide for parents who have English as a second language or who have reading difficulty?
  - Content: do the words convey what is intended?
  - Format/style/tone: is the design and layout attractive and clearly presented; is the style appropriate, e.g. is it patronising, too formal or over-friendly?
  - Balance: are you sending too many or too few written communications to parents – how do you know? Are there other ways of conveying the information?
  - Arrival: how do you know when/if parents have received their communications?

- Participate in the child's adjustment to school: attend meetings of reception teachers and assistants when they are discussing their new children during the first few weeks of admission; offer them a further observation of any child who is giving early cause for concern.

Governors

- Inform yourselves as a governing body: use a governors' meeting to consider all aspects of starting school; request reception teachers and assistants to share their practices with you and invite one or two new parents to offer their views as consumers.
- Attend one of the meetings for new parents: you can offer them information on the role of the governors, particularly the parent governor and also act as observer, providing the head with some evaluation of the meeting based on parental responses.
- Have a 'meet the governors' social occasion for new parents when there is opportunity to talk informally about the school and what parents can expect for their children.
- Budget for minor school improvements which will improve the quality of provision for the reception class, e.g. a separate, fenced-off play area with an outside shed for large apparatus; a covered area for parents with pushchairs meeting their children.

Preschool groups

- Help the local school to gain a clear picture of your provision and practices: prior to a visit from the school send a copy of any documentation that you may have, and a list of the names of children attending. On the day of the visit, provide a plan of your intentions and make arrangements for a time to talk after the session (if not possible immediately after, meet after school).
- Ensure that you have opportunities to visit the reception class in session, preferably both at the beginning and the end of the academic year in order to see the rate of progress of the children. Plan to talk with the teacher after the session in order to clarify any practices that you are not clear about. Be frank in giving your views of where you perceive to be large gaps in continuity, particularly where this might constitute a trauma for certain individuals.

Teachers and teaching assistants

- Find out about the child prior to admission. Try to identify and visit each child's preschool setting. If home visits are not practical for all families, give priority to those children who do not attend a preschool placement. If possible, arrange for teaching assistants to accompany teachers on preschool visits; their early contact with children is as important as it is for the teacher and their observations will supplement the teacher's.
- Encourage preschool settings to offer some similar experiences for children: encourage representatives from different preschool settings to meet together in order to find out more about what each group does; within the constraints of different resources, aim towards some common practices, e.g. expectations, provision and use of equipment, routines.
- Use home visits to

  - gather information: observe the child's *modus operandi* at home, his or her interests and relationships with the family; gather information about the child through friendly discussion with parents rather than using a questionnaire (see Chapter 7);
  - provide information for the parents: talk through the school

Suggested Action contd.
brochure, illustrating it with details of curriculum and organisation; try to respond to parents' concerns rather than offer a
'set piece';
 — provide information for the child: use a photograph album and
   miniature play people and tell the child the story of Bola's
   (substitute child's name) first day in school; the story and
   photographs could include the journey from home, the arrival of
   other children and parents, physical characteristics of the building, including the cloakroom, lavatories, hall and playground;
   personalise the story as much as possible, referring to the names
   of known adults and children from the preschool setting and
   home details, e.g. name of dog; leave one item related to the
   story, e.g. picture-book on the same theme or a photograph, to
   encourage the child to play through this scenario at home;
 — offer resources: take examples of play packs or early reading
   books to leave on loan; use the opportunity to explain the loan
   facilities operating in school.

• Organise 'welcome to school' meetings: plan different occasions
  to meet the needs and preferences of your parents; these may
  include

  — a large formal meeting held in the hall when the headteacher
    and chair of governors talk about the aims of the school;
  — a small informal meeting designed for parents to meet the
    teacher and assistant on a semi-social basis and to learn about
    aspects of classroom life; this may be done through illustrated
    talks or use of video depicting curriculum activities and routines
    such as lunchtimes, playtimes and hall times; communication is
    helped if all parties wear badges on these occasions (these may
    be designed by older children in the school).

• Organise a flexible admission: delay admission to school until
  October: use September to home visit every home; have parent/child
  workshops in you introduce each area of the curriculum in turn
  and encourage handling of resources; explain some school routines to parents, e.g. accessing and returning resources, dressing
  and undressing for PE, procedures for going outside; encourage
  parents to familiarise their children with these routines in the
  school setting.

- Help children to become pupils: establish a small team of teaching assistants (voluntary and paid) who are carefully briefed about aspects of school adjustment. Arrange for the team to work with you during the early weeks of admission. Encourage the team to support children during transition times and during playtimes. In particular, alert them to occasions when children do not understand the teacher's instructions, cannot recognise when they are expected to respond to a question in a group, cannot remember what to do.

  Review each day with your team during the first two weeks of admission; use this time to share observations of those individuals who are finding adjustment difficult; aim to be specific about the difficulties encountered and plan for a key adult to remain close to that child during these times.

  When children transfer to full-time provision, invite parents in to join them for lunch sessions during the first week. Hold a series of weekly surgeries for parents of new children to discuss any perceived and actual adjustment problems.

Parents

- Be clear about your reasons in selecting a school for your child:

  - Be aware that, although modern buildings and spacious class-rooms are attractive, the most valuable resource for your child is his or her teacher and teaching assistant.
  - Give priority to your child attending a local school which makes it more likely that friendships will develop with children who live near home.
  - Visit the school for yourself in order to judge its suitability for your child, rather than rely on messages from neighbours and friends.

- Prepare your child for school: avoid overemphasising the event but help your child to have some understanding of what might happen through stories and through walking past the school building during playtimes; following preschool visits, develop a scrapbook with your child in which he or she draws, paints and sticks pictures from magazines of school events.
- Observe signs of your child's adjustment to school: while instances of fatigue and irritability during the first few weeks are probably to be expected, be alert to signs of distress or prolonged unwillingness

---

Suggested Action contd.
to talk about school life. Do not hesitate to approach the teacher
with these concerns.

REFERENCES

1. Hughes, M., Wikeley, F. and Nash, T. (1994) Parents' choice of school, in A. Pollard and F. Bourne (eds) *Teaching and Learning in the Primary School*. Routledge/The Open University, London.
2. Barratt, G. (1986) *Starting School: An Evaluation of the Experience*. AMMA, University of East Anglia, Norwich.
3. Davie, C.E., Hutt, S.J., Vincent, E. and Mason, M. (1984) *The Young Child at Home*. NFER/Nelson, Slough.
4. Dunn, J. (1989) The family as an educational environment in the pre-school years, *British Journal of Educational Psychology: Early Childhood Education* (Monograph Series no. 4), p. 68.
5. Raven, J. (1990) Parents, education and schooling, in C. Desforges (ed.) *Early Childhood Education*. Scottish Academic Press, Edinburgh, p. 52.
6. Cleave, S., Jowett, S. and Bate, M. (1982) *And So to School*. NFER/Nelson, Slough.
7. Stephenson, C. (1988) *Focus on Four*. Area Advisory Service, Stevenage.
8. Cleave, Jowett and Bate (1982) *op. cit.* (note 6).
9. Thomas, V. (1973) Children's use of language in the nursery, *Educational Research*, Vol. 15, no. 3, pp. 209–16.
10. Woods, D., McMahan, L. and Cranstoun, Y. (1980) *Working with Under-Fives*. Grant McIntyre, London, p. 101.
11. Sylva, K., Roy, C. and Painter, M. (1980) *Child Watching at Playgroup and Nursery School*. Grant McIntyre, London.
12. Tizard, B. and Hughes, M. (1984) *Young Children Learning*. Fontana, London.
13. Department of Education and Science (DES) (1988a) *Our Changing Schools*. HMSO, London. DES (1992) *Reporting Pupils' Achievement to Parents* (Circular 5/92, April). DES, London.
14. Cleave, Jowett and Bate (1982) *op. cit.* (note 6).
15. Cousins, J. (1990) Are your little Humpty Dumpties floating or sinking? What sense do children of four make of the reception class at school? *Early Years*, Vol. 10, no. 2, Spring, pp. 28–38.
16. Cleave, Jowett and Bate (1982) *op. cit.* (note 6).
17. Sharp, C. (1987) Local education authority admission policies and practices, in *Four Year Olds in School: Policy and Practice*. NFER/SCDC, Slough.
18. Cousins (1990) *op. cit.* (note 15).
19. Pre-School Playgroups Association and British Association for Early Childhood Education (1985) *Four Year Olds but Not Yet Five*. BAECE, London.
20. West, A., Banfield, S. and Varlaam, A. (1990) Evaluation of an early entry to infant school pilot exercise, *Research Papers in Education*, Vol. 5, no. 5, p. 244.
21. Willes, M.J. (1983) *Children into Pupils*. Routledge & Kegan Paul, London.

22. Cook-Gumperz, J. (1986) The social construction of literacy, in *Studies in Interaction of Sociolinguistics*, Vol. 3. p. 60. Cambridge University Press.
23. Jackson, M. (1987) Making sense of school, in A. Pollard (ed.) *Children and their Primary Schools*. Falmer Press, Lewes.
24. *Ibid.*, p. 83.
25. Barratt (1986) *op. cit.* (note 2).
26. Sinclair, J.McH. and Coulthard, R.M. (1975) *Towards an Analysis of Discourse: The English Used by Teachers and Pupils*. Oxford University Press, London.
27. Willes (1983) *op. cit.* (note 21), p. 129.
28. Cousins (1990) *op. cit.* pp. 22–38.
29. Willes (1983) *op. cit.* (note 21).
30. *Ibid.*, p. 186.
31. Ghaye, A. and Pascal, C. (1988) Four-year-old children in reception classrooms: participant perceptions and practice, *Educational Studies*, Vol. 14, no. 2, pp. 187–208.

3

THE PERSONAL DEVELOPMENT
OF YOUNG CHILDREN

Education of young children is concerned with all aspects of development. The way in which the child develops and matures in the affective domain is as important as, and closely linked to, intellectual development. His or her happiness and sense of well-being and the quality of the child's relationships will particularly affect his or her ability to learn.

The uniqueness of young children is well known to every early years teacher. Because 4- and 5-year-olds are relatively unsocialised and because of their limited experience, their individual characteristics are very noticeable during their initial months in the classroom. Every child arrives at school with his or her particular collection of beliefs, fears, hopes, attitudes and skills. These are some of the features that comprise individual social, personal and emotional development. The child's personal characteristics influence how the child approaches life. This is partly linked to intellectual capacities but more often it is to do with such qualities as resilience, humour, empathy, tolerance and confidence. Above all, it is founded on the way in which the child views him or herself. This chapter explores some of the factors which affect children personally both before they move to school and during their first year as a pupil.

SELF-CONCEPT

Each person's self-concept is closely linked with the view that person believes others to have of him or her. The perceived views of those close to the individual are considered particularly influential and these persons are deemed the significant others. Because of their immaturity, young children are particularly open to the opinions and views of others. As children grow up and begin to develop their own value systems, the views of other adults start to be less influential: the 8-year-old starts to look to peers more for approval although, once formed, self-images are difficult to alter.

However, the preschool child's sense of self-worth is heavily dependent on the regard shown to the child by family and carers. Neil Bolton stresses the importance of having 'shared concerns' within the family. He refers to the sensitive ways in which mothers interpret and tune in to their very young child's early body language and suggests that it is this interconnectedness that encourages further responses and initiates later intended communication. The child's identity and urge to develop is strengthened through the parent's personal involvement.[1] Coopersmith's study of parent–child relationships illustrates this vividly, but also reminds us of the consequences when this involvement is not present.[2] Coopersmith followed a group of middle-class boys from primary school into adolescence and found that, on the basis of tests, teacher ratings and self-ratings, they divided into three clear groups with 'high', 'medium' and 'low' self-esteem. The first group were largely successful both in social and learning achievements. They were confident, at ease with themselves and able to evaluate their own abilities. The second group of boys had some of these characteristics but were less self-assured and more inclined to seek the approval of adults and other children. The 'low' self-esteem group were significantly different. They were fearful and hesitant, under-rated their abilities and were unable to relate to others. Coopersmith concluded that there was in fact no evidence of any differences in ability or physical attractiveness between the groups. The main cause appeared to be with the families. The first group had parents who listened to them, respected their views and made them feel that they mattered. They also treated their children consistently and were considered by the boys to be 'fair'. Conversely, the latter group came from families who appeared to take little interest in them and in their achievements, and who treated the boys in an unpredictable manner. Although this study is limited in class and gender, other studies re-enforce these findings in different groups.[3]

The structure and stability of family life can also affect how children view themselves. The range of family patterns varies enormously. Young children may come from single-parent families, from a partnership where parents are cohabiting or from step-families where one parent has remarried. Although most children under 5 years still live with two natural parents, it may be assumed that marital disharmony exists in many of these households before the break-up of the partnership.[4]

Hetherington's study found that the effects of divorce vary considerably with the child's age when the separation takes place. Preschool children are upset but do not understand what is happening, as do children in middle childhood.[5] There is no predictable long-term outcomes for children of separated and divorced parents, although longitudinal studies in America suggest that some children continue to feel unwanted, damaged and insecure through to adulthood.[6,7] Others survive the experience well and serve to support Penelope Leach's suggestion that we need to be objective when considering what meets people's needs: 'Rising divorce rates are discussed in terms of "broken homes" and "lone parents"; the role of soaring remarriage rates and informal partnerships in mending some of those homes and hearts is scarcely considered.'[8] Despite this, reception teachers as well often witness and deal with children who are distressed, confused and rejected as a result of family turbulence.

Parents, then, have a powerful effect on each child's sense of self-worth during the early school years. Where home relationships are unsatisfactory or even damaging, the child's first teacher has the heavy responsibility of trying to repair this damage.

Susan Fountain reports the findings of a group of primary teachers who identified behaviours they considered to characterise children with positive self-esteem. These included a realistic assessment of their own work; recognition of the worth of others, including giving them positive feedback; the ability to accept constructive criticism; the ability to work co-operatively in a group, accepting the contributions of each member; and the ability to react reasonably and assertively in a conflict situation.[9] Manifestations of these behaviours are very evident in reception-age children, who feel secure in themselves. On the other hand, behaviour problems may reflect a poor self-esteem and children who seek attention in negative ways have a particular need for praise and recognition.

SELF-ESTEEM ON STARTING SCHOOL

Any adult who has started a new job has just some idea of the excitement, trepidation and anxiety experienced by the novice in school. Even the most confident child can find the move to school intimidating. We have already described the range of new experiences to be faced and the potential discontinuities with life at home, nursery or playgroup. The process of 'settling' into school involves a plethora of feelings. The reception-age children in Gill Barratt's study recognised and described some of these feelings when looking at some pictures. Although responses reflected individual viewpoints, they commonly identified experiences of being scared, shy, bored or upset and not knowing what to do. Some also recognised the fear of getting things 'wrong', of home sickness and of fatigue.[10] Most of these feelings can be linked to not feeling in control. Barratt's study showed that, partly because of the way the pupil role is perceived by young children (based on what they have learnt from parents, peers and the media), they will often adopt a passive attitude, be reluctant to take risks in their learning and be anxious about their inadequacies being revealed. The fear of being wrong is a major inhibitor. Barratt suggested that too often in mainstream schools there was still emphasis placed on children needing to do things correctly and that children do need to feel that it is safe and acceptable not to know something.[11] This message remains as powerful today, as it is a keystone to building children's confidence in learning.

While some children adjust quickly to school, others feel themselves to be passive recipients of a strange new culture. In conversations with teachers, parents might say that they don't recognise their child at school. One parent said desperately 'he doesn't shut up at home and yet you can't get a peep out of him here'. This behaviour may apply to a number of newcomers as they find their feet but, eventually, this type of comment warns that an individual possibly feels out of his or her depth. The teacher really does need to move close to the child in every way at this time. In order to read the child, the adult must be able to decentre and place him or herself in the child's shoes. What does the child make of the experience that is being offered? Does the child hear what that teacher is saying to him or her? Can the child make sense of the pattern of the school day? The problem is compounded if the child's previous home experiences have not supported him or her as a person. When a 4-year-old starts school as one of a large class, underachievement is a possibility. Where that 4-year-old has already received powerful messages from home that the child isn't important and that no one really cares about him or her, where that results in the child becoming withdrawn in class and so not easy for the teacher to read and recognise his or her abilities; in these circumstances underachievement is a distinct probability.

SELF-ESTEEM AND MOTIVATION

Although the child's self-concept is formed through early experience it can also affect motivation and the drive to learn. Prior to coming to school children will have learnt a great deal in their own way, through curiosity and investigation, through trial and error and through imitation (see also Chapter 4). Most will have continued this style of learning in preschool settings. In short, children have learnt mainly because of the urge to do so.

Studies concerned with intrinsic motivation have found that the experience of school usually means a lessening of this self-imposed urge to learn and an increase in extrinsic motivation.[12] This is largely attributed to the greater degree of control that is exerted over the child as he or she learns to become one of a group. The decline in intrinsic motivation will be most noticeable in classrooms which stress high levels of teacher control, competition and comparisons between children. Deci and Ryan highlight how the classroom environment has an effect on intrinsic motivation and make a useful distinction between controlling and informational environments. A controlling environment means that the pupil is dependent on the teacher: the teacher decides on what is to be learnt and assesses whether the learning objectives have been successfully achieved. An informational environment is one where the pupil is encouraged to plan his or her own learning to use available resources to develop this learning and to take some responsibility for assessing achievement.[13] Studies indicate[14] and are re-enforced by my observations of classrooms that children perceived to be less able receive a higher level of teacher control than those regarded as more able. In reception classes this can include the less able group having more direct instruction on basic numeracy and literacy skills and fewer opportunities for play. While the teacher understandably wishes to monitor the progress of these children closely, it is important that this should be balanced by opportunities for them to experience self-directed activity. The children who are regarded as having learning difficulties (who may in fact simply be the younger and less mature element in the class) should not be penalised by having a more restricted curriculum on account of them needing to accelerate their achievement in recording symbols.

REWARDS

The notion of controlling and informational environments can be extended to the ways in which children are rewarded in the classroom. The controlling teacher will regularly use extrinsic rewards to control behaviour and achievement. Star charts, stickers and prizes will be awarded for success. Conversely, the teacher in the informational environment will help the child to see the value of what the child has done and to appreciate what the child has achieved. This teacher feedback will include encouragement and praise rather than external rewards. It is important that this praise is not indiscriminate and that it does help the child to see how he or she is progressing. Margaret Donaldson also wisely points out that 'it is a subtle art to give genuine information and to encourage at the same time'.[15] She also distinguishes between rewards which are external to the activity tackled and recognition, which is part of every person's need to share achievements with others.[16]

Researchers reveal that, where activities are rewarded by extrinsic prizes, there is less likelihood of the activity being continued and enjoyed for its own sake when these prizes are withdrawn. In one study in a nursery school, a group of children were provided with drawing materials and told that they would receive a prize for drawing which, in due course, they did. Another group were given the same materials but there was no mention of prizes. Some time after, drawing was provided as one of a range of optional activities; significantly, the children who chose to spend the least time on drawing were those who had been previously rewarded.[17]

Most early years teachers fortunately recognise the value of offering praise and recognition rather than competitive awards. They also strive to achieve an informational environment, sometimes working against major odds of large numbers of children and inadequate staffing. Unfortunately, the downward pressures of the National Curriculum have caused some teachers to impose tighter controls on children's learning as a response to the demand for accountability and the raising of standards. Likely outcomes of this are increased stress levels for both teacher and children, and the danger of invidious comparisons being made between individual's achievements. Pepitone warns that 'Competition becomes more powerful as the stakes become higher; the fun and games of early childhood often turn to deadly contests. By definition, where rewards are limited, some must be losers'.[18]

It is, of course, quite possible to create the impression of high standards of competency. Young children are very ready to please and will acquire short-term mastery of facts through imitation, regular practice and repetition. While this performance may impress a lay person it is highly likely that only an image of learning is being seen, with children having no real understanding of what they are required to regurgitate. It is essential that, during the first year in school, children are given opportunities to demonstrate what they know already and to use the learning strategies that are familiar to them. If this does not happen and young children are required to be in an environment and respond to teacher demands which do not make sense to them, Barratt suggests that this can result in some individuals withdrawing their preparedness to participate in learning and that this can be the first step towards early disaffection.[19] Annabel Dixon, an experienced early years teacher, stresses that this state can be manifested in different types of behaviour including dreaminess, listlessness, hesitancy and awkwardness as well as anti-social responses.[20] These descriptions are only too easily recognisable for every reception teacher. Importantly, such negative attitudes are the beginning of the child distancing him or herself from school and the probable downward spiral of achievement.

TEACHER EXPECTATIONS

The young child's first teacher is very important to him or her and comes within the category of the significant other. It follows that the teacher's expectations of the child not only influences how the child views him or herself but also have a causal affect on the child's achievements. If a child believes that the teacher has a low opinion of the child's competence, the likely result is a drop in confidence and motivation, which result in poor performance.

Cooper distinguishes between self-fulfilling prophecies and sustaining expectations. He suggests that the self-fulfilling prophecy occurs when an inaccurate expectation of an individual has subsequently influenced the behaviour of that individual so as to make the expectation accurate. A sustaining expectation follows an initially accurate judgement, which is maintained despite other influences.[21] As we shall see, a self-fulfilling prophecy can lead to an expectation of a child which is sustained in later years.

Potentially, the new entrant to school is at risk of self-fulfilling prophecies. In the absence of skilled observations and sound background information about the child's past experiences, the reception teacher is more likely to make an inaccurate judgement about a child's abilities and potential for learning. Furthermore, without any other information, the teacher's judgement may be unduly influenced by the child's social competencies rather than what he or she can actually do. A consequent halo effect can operate and cause both overoptimistic and pessimistic views of children. This can operate in various ways. One Scottish study of multicultural nursery schools suggests that, in the absence of detailed observations of individual children, teachers made assessments of them based on their ethnic-group membership. Thus a quiet, hardworking and well behaved Asian child's difficulties with language were overlooked.[22] In other circumstances, the child who is polite and socially at ease can be regarded as generally able: the child who is awkward with people, who finds conversation difficult or who speaks colloquially, may be judged to be of more limited ability. Gordon Wells argues strongly that 'Any suggestion that working-class children as a whole are "disadvantaged" in any absolute or irrevocable sense because their home experience leads them to use language differently, is certainly not appropriate'.[23]

In reality, of course, many early years teachers make shrewd and accurate judgements about their children based on good knowledge of child development and their own professional knowledge. However, the argument is strengthened for a sensitive and formative assessment of individuals when they enter school in order to avoid the dangers of children being stuck with wrong labels for which they eventually settle.

Fortunately, though, it seems that the young child's general optimism initially shields him or her against the effects of low teacher expectations. The drop in motivation is thought to occur when the teacher's low expectations are effectively communicated to the pupil, who then believes that his or her failure is inevitable and there is nothing to be done about it. Two studies indicate that a 4- or 5-year-old does not necessarily link failure to lack of ability.[24,25] He or she is more likely to believe that he or she might succeed in another situation, or if he or she tries harder. It is only as the child grows older and begins to link failure to lack of ability and is aware that this conforms with the teacher's view of him or her that the child settles for achieving little. The child's next teacher will view this dampened attainment and both teacher's and child's expectations will sustain the status quo. Rogers warns that, although we may not immediately see the effects of the reception teacher's expectations, they can be critical for what happens later in school.[26]

POTENTIAL INSECURITIES

Tina Bruce suggests that having a clear sense of who you are is closely linked with self-esteem and that children from minority groups will find

this difficult if they are labelled by others.[27] Many 4-year-olds are still
sorting out their own identity; certain groups of young children will find
starting school particularly difficult if their sense of self-worth is still
insecure and has been jeopardised on the grounds of class, race, gender
or ability. The reception teacher's task is to aim to strengthen each child's
self-image to provide a resilience against bias and prejudice.

We have already seen how teacher expectations can affect children's
view of themselves as achievers and their subsequent motivation. And
yet, as Val Wood states, teacher expectations are grounded in their own
background and upbringing. The danger suggested earlier that teachers
may place too much emphasis on children's social skills when judging
overall abilities is compounded by Wood's warning that teachers may
spot ability in middle-class children more easily than they do in children
from less advantaged backgrounds, simply because they are more attuned
to the former.[28] Moreover, children from backgrounds that include books
and conversations are likely to find the move to school easier than others.
When the child finds him or herself in a setting very different from home,
the adjustments to be made will be considerable.

Similarly, children from ethnic minority groups may also have their
behaviour misinterpreted or their abilities underestimated on grounds of
their difficulties with English as a second language. Children who are
facing a new culture as well as being a newcomer to school will need
time to accustom. However, reflection and puzzlement may be considered
to be sulky and uncommunicative behaviour. Misunderstandings about
the needs of children from different ethnic groups may arise because
of lack of acceptance or understanding of the cultural and linguistic
background. Mary Willes, writing in the 1980s, describes the typical
difficulties of a 5-year-old who has English as a second language, who
does not easily understand her teacher and is not able to make herself
understood; in this case the start of literacy is dependent on learning
a new language and there are few or no opportunities for the child to
develop the mother-tongue language that are usually available in the
first year of schooling.[29] It is worrying that, ten years later, those
schools with a significant number of bilingual pupils having achieved
some financial support for specialist help are now in danger of losing
it. Additionally, there sadly remain classrooms described by Willes as
monolingual, where the presence of bilingual children becomes a problem
that tends to be ignored once children have grasped English approximate
to their peers.[30]

The reception teacher is in a crucial position to re-enforce each child's self-image. This involves positively acknowledging and respecting aspects of their race, culture and class. If a child is not encouraged to use his or her home language or talk about aspects of his or her lifestyle, then an important aspect of individuality is being ignored.

If children are truly seen as individuals, everyone can be regarded as having special needs. However, the majority of children should be able to learn and progress within the curriculum offered. Those who have particular difficulties are required to have special educational provision made for them. The 1994 Act identifies learning difficulty if the child:

> has a significantly greater difficulty in learning than the majority of children of the same age;
> has a disability which either prevents or hinders the child from making use of educational facilities of a kind provided for children of the same age in schools within the area of the local education authority.[31]

However, since the inception of the Warnock Report there has been an increased awareness that in all classes there is a continuum of need. Between the extremes of very able children and those who are clear candidates for statementing there are children who have a range of learning needs in some aspect of learning at some point in their school careers. We should all accept that some children do find some aspects of school difficult, and sometimes the onus is not on the child but on the school to consider change. Warnock reminds us that

> Some handicapping conditions, particularly behaviour disorders, may be brought about, or accentuated by factors at the school such as its premises, organisation or staff. In such cases assessment may need to focus on the institution, the classroom setting or the teacher, as well as the individual child and his family if it is to encompass a full consideration of the child's problems and their educational implications.[32]

For a child who finds learning difficult, the need for a positive and supportive reception to school is paramount. Such children are likely to find school adjustment particularly problematic and will be confused by the responses of more able children as well as the demands of the adult. The reception class teacher is in a special position of having to diagnose some of the learning difficulties that only clearly emerge when the child arrives at school. He or she will offer support by allowing increased opportunities for less able children to learn at their own pace, to apply their understandings and develop social skills through play and conversations. This type of modified curriculum will more likely establish a better foundation for progress than an additional focus on numeracy and literacy, which is intended to accelerate development.

All children will benefit from opportunities to apply their learning. Self-esteem and confidence increase and learning is strengthened in situations when knowledge is demonstrated in practical activity. This is particularly important for children with learning difficulties who need every chance to experience the pleasure and surge of motivation that comes with success.

EARLY SOCIAL AND MORAL INFLUENCES

Young children learn how to regard and relate to others initially within their homes. Most children grow up in families, many of which we have seen undergo marked changes even during the early years. Contact with friends, relatives, neighbours and preschool groups increase the child's experience of people and broaden the mesh of observations that provide the child with his or her model of how people behave in life.

Children may learn in the home how to behave differently as boys and girls and will take these beliefs about sex-appropriate behaviour into the classroom. Families do appear to treat their sons and daughters in different ways. One study of 5-year-olds shows that all members of the family encouraged girls to dance, dress up and to play quietly while boys were given blocks and trucks and allowed boisterous play. Both girls and boys were actively discouraged from what was considered inappropriate behaviour for their sex.[33] Morgan and Dunn point out that children will arrive at school having already learnt a great deal about how society treats men and women. Role expectations will have been set at home and, given a large class of children, the teacher's easiest means of management control will be to follow the children's expectations of these roles. However, if this happens the authors stress that 'during the early years at school they will almost inevitably become resolutely set in a framework which makes explicit the different expectations of the two sexes and continues the vicious circle of deeply engendered biases in adult behaviour and instincts'.[34]

Because young children will absorb, imitate and quickly adapt the attitudes of their parents, there is equal danger of some children demonstrating racism. Most have grasped the notion of racial identity by the age of 4 years and, if they perceive other ethnic groups to be different from themselves, they tend to have negative views of them.[35] However, although attitudes may be well established these are not necessarily manifested in behaviour. Goodman found that her 4-year-olds were very reluctant publicly to demonstrate their beliefs about race.[36] A later example quoted by Robert Jeffcoate recounts how a head of a nursery used photographs of black persons to stimulate discussion with her children. In one group she led discussion focusing on attributes other than race and skin colour. In a further group, children were simply observed using the photographs. The outcomes in this group were worryingly different. In the first group there was no reference to colour and no disparaging racial remarks were made, whilst in the second group, when left to their own devices, children made such negative and derisory comments about black people that the headteacher was required to intervene.[37] These examples point up the seriousness of the issue. In some schools teachers must face up to the harsh realities of children's lives in the outside world and help them to develop their own moral frameworks. Without attributing blame or confronting the children, teachers have the hard job of modifying attitudes.

For those children who may face racial abuse outside school, it is even more important that teachers try to prepare them for such events and aim for a positive classroom climate and group convictions based on tolerance and interest. These should be so clearly communicated to the children that they offer some protective armour.

Another major source of influence for many children is television. An NFER study in 1986 reported that it was the one single activity on which children under 5 spend the most time.[38] Gammage reports that British and Canadian children observed in his studies watched television for between 20 and 25 hours a week.[39] The affects of this have not been studied closely and the optimist will have faith that, as with other experiences, children will actively process their viewing in order to make sense of it. Winick and Winick comment that 'a young viewer can relate only to what her development has made it possible to understand'.[40] Clearly the dangers lie in indiscriminate viewing. Some television programmes for young children, such as *You and Me* and *Sesame Street*, have aimed to offer positive models of ethnic-minority groups and disabled people. Studies have shown that these programmes have positive effects on attitudes towards race and disability.[41] However, increasingly teachers report seeing worrying signs of disturbance in young children who have been exposed to sex and violence following the viewing of television and video programmes.[42] We can assume that television can have an effect on young children's social development both for good and ill. Parents have an important role to play in determining these effects through monitoring viewing. Studies also indicate that children are most strongly influenced by television programmes which are not counterbalanced by anything they have experienced at home.[43] This implies the need for adults to demonstrate and discuss with children their own values and attitudes which help children make sense of what they view.

SOCIAL DEVELOPMENTS

We have already seen some of the complex requirements on the individual when he or she comes to school. A successful adjustment will also heavily depend on each child's social abilities and the way in which the child is able to relate to other adults and children. OFSTED stresses that the quality of children's relationships are central for forming children's attitudes to co-operation, social behaviour and self-discipline.[44] This, of course, implies a classroom environment in which children are able, and encouraged, to demonstrate these attitudes. There is sound evidence to show that young children are naturally kind, and by 4 and 5 years they do show positive social behaviour, such as helping, comforting and supporting others in their group.[45] Further studies show that this behaviour is strengthened both through praise and encouragement and through adults demonstrating similar approaches.[46]

MAKING FRIENDS

One important factor which relates to children feeling settled in school is the ability to make friends. Studies indicate that the well adjusted 4-year-old should be able to negotiate several peer relationships with ease. Moreover at this age, children regard friends as very important. One small-scale study demonstrated that when a number of children in a kindergarten left for their new school both the group transferring and the group left behind showed signs of negative behaviour and mild distress. Although the researcher admits that the agitation demonstrated from the leaving group may have been due to the anticipated transfer, the group of children remaining appeared to have missed their 'friends' after they had gone.[47]

   The need for friends is, of course, a central human need and lack of friends can have important consequences for later success in school. For instance, different studies consistently link the lack of ability to make friends to later school dropout.[48]

Young children arrive at school very differently equipped to relate to others. It is a sad but evident truth that some children are more popular than others. One contributory factor may be physical looks. One study showed that preschool children who were regarded as physically attractive by their peers tended to be regarded as more desirable as friends. This link was more noticeable for girls.[49] Children also move towards making friends with those who are similar to themselves. Thus the popularity of an individual child may be affected by the child being in a peer group with others of the same ethnic origin, the same sex or with those of a similar ability.[50] However, apart from these factors, Rubin's study of preschool children suggests that there are important and complex social skills involved in making friends. These include the ability to gain entry to group activities; to be approving and supportive of one's peers; to manage conflicts appropriately; and to exercise sensitivity and tact.[51] Popular children were particularly adept in using these skills of friendship.

As with adult friendships, it seems that the more young children put into a relationship, the more they will gain from it. Rubin's own work and his reference to other studies show that the children who make friends easily are those who involve others in their play, who praise them, show affection and are attentive to their needs. Rubin stressed, however, that successful 'friendly behaviour' only occurs when it is seen as appropriate by the child receiving it. Some individuals do not succeed in relating to others when their approaches are regarded as too timid or overeffusive.

In order to maintain a friendship children also learn to reconcile arguments, recognise when others are upset and take steps to help them.

Rubin's work indicates that, before children come to school, most will have learnt a great deal about relating to others. In preschool settings children experience both rejection and acceptance by their peers and so gradually understand what is required in being considered as a friend and in maintaining that friendship. Family life will also significantly influence social development. Where children have from a young age been involved in communicating with brothers and sisters and other children of family friends, they are likely to be socially a step ahead of their peers who have not had this experience.

Even before this, though, some children may have personality traits which significantly hinder or help the development of relationships. An American study found that babies as young as 12 weeks displayed body symptoms which seemed to be indicators of personality. Using measures of physical activity, adaptability, sensitivity and disposition, individuals were identified in three groups: easy (flexible and with positive traits); difficult (slow to adapt and negative in mood); and 'slow to warm up' (characterised by sluggish activity, withdrawal from new situations and some negative responses). The continuing study of these babies suggest that these early seeds of personality remain constant as children develop into adolescence. In particular, they were evident when the three groups started school when the 'easy' children socialised much more readily than those in the other two groups.[52] Although this study stresses that the ways in which parents handled their children helped to influence behaviour, it does suggest that some individuals may be better equipped from birth to make friends than others.

Most children learn to negotiate relationships and establish friendships at an early stage in their school career. It is very noticeable when this does not happen, and the young child who is socially isolated is very likely to be unhappy at school. However, it is important to recognise when 'aloneness' is a matter of choice rather than necessity. A 4-year-old may have all the social skills to communicate and play with others but may still choose to spend some time alone. Teachers quickly learn to distinguish between that autonomous behaviour and that demonstrated by the child who is longing but unable to relate to her peers.

Scarlett's study of nursery children suggests that socially isolated children spend a considerable amount of time 'on the sideline' watching others at play. When they do become involved they are necessarily inexperienced participants and they require direction from other children. This can mean that they are devalued as members of the group.[53] Both Rubin's and Scarlett's work suggests that the adult can play a part in helping some children to acquire the necessary skills for developing positive relationships.

DEVELOPMENT OF HUMOUR

One of the joys of early years teaching is the fun that is engendered in the classroom. Studies have shown that humour in young children both affects and is affected by other aspects of growth. Although Rubin does not identify a sense of humour as a specific requirement in making friends, he does suggest that from the youngest age the ability to smile, laugh and to have a sense of fun will invite positive responses from others.[54] In regard to intellectual development, Chapman and Foot found that children will only find things amusing if they understand them well.[55] Athey supports this and further suggests that it makes sense, therefore, to have opportunities for children to play around with these understandings which, in turn, lead to increased confidence and competence.[56]

Humour is also linked to creativity. In their book on children's humour, McGhee and Chapman reported studies that have shown that creative children of 5 and 6 years are more spontaneous and playful than those who are not so creative. They suggest that the following sequence of events can be traced in this relationship between humour and creativity. Children who are curious are most likely to engage in fantasy. These 'flights of fantasy' are so often at odds with the real world that they are seen as funny. As children enjoy the humour of their fantasy, they increase their abilities in divergent thinking and develop their sense of humour. Classroom studies at high-school level report that a humorous class atmosphere was responsible for higher scores on tests of creativity which focused on divergent thinking.[57] Although there is no similar early years classroom study it seems reasonable to assume that fun and laughter will encourage young children to relax and be inventive. Tina Bruce suggests that child-initiated or 'free-flo' play where children mix, match and rearrange experiences offers a good context for humorous activity.[58]

Following from the high-school classroom studies on humour and creativity, Ziv suggested four priorities for teachers.[59] The first was to develop an atmosphere of humour in the classroom. This is largely achieved by the reception teacher demonstrating a sense of fun, gentle teasing, smiles and an ability to laugh at small mistakes. Secondly, to use humour to promote a breakaway from ordinary, conventional outcomes. In early years classrooms this can be by encouraging children to play with and invent words or create story endings which are funny and sometimes ludicrous. Thirdly, the teacher demonstrates a sense of humour which then becomes infectious among the children. Ziv's final suggestion, which is for the teacher to instruct children to use humour, is certainly not appropriate for early years practice. However, young children will respond to models of behaviour and these are particularly effective when offered through stories. Children of 4 and 5 years will laugh delightedly at stories which contain elements of surprise and unpredictable behaviour. Cathy Nutbrown recounts how, having listened to stories about disguise in *Elmer* and *Harry the Dirty Dog*, children used dressing-up clothes and masks and different voices to surprise and amuse their friends and parents.[60]

It is important for the teacher to be aware of the level of humour that is accessible for this age-group. Clearly, sophisticated riddles and jokes are not going to be understood, whereas shared understandings of story content and enjoyment of first-hand experiences of humorous events provide opportunities for learning through pleasure and enable children to see the 'funny side of life'.

GLOBAL UNDERSTANDING

The term 'global' is used to describe the child's emerging understanding of a diverse world outside, and the many issues and problems which are involved in enabling all people to live in harmony together and to receive a 'fair deal' in life.

These concepts, far from being remote, are experienced at a personal level daily in school. Young infant children are regularly involved in issues of fairness and discrimination, sharing of resources, environmental issues, aggression and resolution and application of rules for living. The use and discussion of these experiences will sow seeds of understanding which can be explored at a deeper level at a later stage in school life.

Children need to know about their own culture and traditions and to be sure that these are acknowledged and appreciated in school. Clearly, some children experience a home culture and values which parallel those in school. Other children lead different home lives. Suggestions which enable these children to accommodate two different cultural lifestyles include: ensuring opportunities for positive identification with both cultural (and ethnic) communities; equal value being placed on both forms of language used; and the importance of both lifestyles and cultures being capable of change.[61]

When children feel sure that their own culture is recognised in school, given the opportunity, they will readily show interest in other lifestyles and cultures. This is easier to foster in areas which accommodate families from a rich mix of cultural backgrounds. However, in all localities children can be helped to develop attitudes of tolerance and interest in others, based on an appreciation of similarities and differences between people.

MORAL DEVELOPMENT

The young child's moral behaviour is largely demonstrated through his or her relationships with others and thus is closely linked to the child's social development. However, the child's understandings about right and wrong, fairness and justice, is part of development in thinking. As children start to have views about these issues and make moral judgements, these will guide their social behaviour and eventually help to establish values. In one definition values are established by the ability to choose freely, in an informed way, from a range of alternative options; viewing your values positively and openly sharing your views with others; and reflecting your values in your actions persistently so that they begin to reflect the way you live.[62] As with other areas of development, children will be at different stages of understanding. Piaget's work, which has been confirmed by later studies,[63] suggests that young children under 5 are not aware of rules for governing behaviour. More mature 5-year-olds will begin to understand rules but only as regulations imposed from outside rather than co-operative agreements. While recognising this level of understanding, by encouraging children to work together, discuss and make decisions, the teacher will be able to help them towards a notion of how rules might be mutually agreed.

Piaget also suggested that 4- and 5-year-olds based their moral judgement on the seriousness of an outcome as opposed to the intention behind it. However, this has been questioned and more recent studies show that young children are capable of more sophisticated understandings. They are able to recognise when an outcome is purely accidental rather than intentional: they are also able to distinguish between breaking pure social conventions (not hanging your coat up) and violating moral conventions (hitting another child).[64]

Once again the classroom environment is crucial for helping to strengthen children's moral judgements. The teacher will use children's own experiences as well as narrative and stories to encourage shared reflections on people's behaviour and motives.

SPIRITUAL DEVELOPMENT

There has been almost no study of young children's spiritual development and little guidance on how spirituality should be fostered in school. What follows is simply a personal view of what may be appropriate.

While social and moral development are concerned with relationships, behaviour and attitudes, spiritual growth concerns beliefs and the recognition of the quality and significance of life. Although this appears an ambitious target for 4- and 5-year-olds, the receptiveness of this age-group is a very positive starter. Young children view many aspects of daily life in a spontaneous and appreciative way and constantly remind adults of the joy of being alive. Thus although any notions of deity and spirituality may be hazy and remote, a major part of the early years programme will offer children experiences which invoke awe and wonder and the opportunity to celebrate. Spiritual development should emphasise the positive factors in living but, at the same time, help children gradually to become aware of some harsh realities, such as separation, illness and death. Role play is an important way in which young children can learn to cope with some difficult situations in life. As Singer and Singer suggest, 'Imaginative play is fun, but in the midst of the joys of making believe, children may also be preparing for the reality of more effective lives'.[65]

Spiritual is not synonymous with religious, and a spiritual dimension can be fostered in most aspects of school life. Moreover, although a collective act of worship should foster spiritual development, this is not legally required until the child is of statutory school age. During the first year the introduction to whole-school worship should be gradual and should only take place when the occasion is particularly geared towards young children.

An environment which nurtures spirituality is closely linked to an ethos, which will include an aesthetically pleasing setting and adults and children who demonstrate respect and care for each other. However, young children will also need specific occasions when they are encouraged to talk about their feelings and to listen to others. They need to be helped to appreciate non-material dimensions, and time to reflect and be quiet in order to learn to welcome silence as a positive factor in life. Most important, children need to feel secure in themselves in order eventually to learn to trust in their own beliefs. This serves to emphasise yet again the importance of each child having a positive self-concept.

Suggested action

Headteacher

- Promote working conditions that enable the staff to feel valued. This is likely to result in all adults valuing the children. Write down three ways in which your school raises the self-concept of the adults working there.
- Develop a whole-school behaviour policy which is based on rewarding positive behaviour and fostering individual self-esteem.

- Provide inservice opportunities for all adults working with the reception class to check how personal development is fostered during the first year in school, e.g. through the curriculum and routines, through playtimes and lunchtimes, through the behaviour and management strategies of adults, through working with parents.
- Ensure that parents are clearly informed about the school's aims for fostering personal development: invite parents to small-group meetings in which you share views on behaviour, values and beliefs. You may never achieve a consensus, but open discussion may help all parties to review their own standpoint.

Governors

- The governing body should be in a strong position to evaluate the climate for personal development in the school. Elect one governor with responsibility for this aspect, who will track children's development during their first year in school. The following areas of observation may be useful:

  - Identify the quiet children in class and not how well engaged they are with various activities (is the withdrawal caused by disaffection or simply shyness?).
  - Identify the socially isolated children; how do teachers help them to 'mix'?
  - Observe playtimes and lunchtimes; note how well children play together and how this is fostered by supervisory assistants.
  - Check how well the outside environment supports young children's personal development, e.g. provision of seating, quiet areas, interest corners containing attractive plants, and rotting logs with four minibeasts.
  - Observe how and when teachers encourage children to talk about their feelings and to empathise with the feelings of others.
  - Observe how well the school introduces young children to aspects of beauty.
  - In conversations with reception teachers, note how well they appear to know their children's personal characteristics. Check this against your own observations of some individual children.

Preschool groups

- Help children to view themselves positively: display photographs of

Suggested Action contd.
all children or, in a non-purpose-built setting, provide a transportable board which has changing displays of photographs or self-portraits of some of the children; discuss the features of those displayed and encourage children to observe similarities and differences.

• Resource and foster situations which encourage children to explore and re-enact emotions, e.g. share the story of *Little Monster* (André Deutch, 1989). The little girl in the story is normally well behaved but she becomes very angry when her mother appears to favour her naughty little brother; discuss these feelings with your children, resource the role-play area and suggest that some of them might like to play through the story.

• Your observations of each child's personal qualities and characteristics will be valued by the receiving teacher; check how much you know about each child under the headings outlined in this chapter. Focus on those individuals who are less well known to you. Try to establish a pen-portrait of each child which you can share with the teacher.

Teachers and teaching assistants

• Create a class climate to promote high self-esteem:

   – Consider how your spoken and body language can effect individuals, e.g. pursed lip, tensed body, toe tapping and abrupt tone communicates irritability/anger; a genuine smile, relaxed body posture, eye contact and warm voice communicates approachability and friendliness.

   – Do not interrupt children when they are speaking; try to interpret hidden messages and assist where there are hesitancies without cutting across the child's thinking.

   – Make a particular effort with difficult children, e.g. find a way of praising the child for something daily; develop a home/school booklet in which to record positive actions in school and agree with parents a system of rewards; keep a special puppet who registers sadness and pleasure in response to the child's behaviour; demonstrate to all your children that you expect them to 'fly high'; they will do their best to respond.

• Use games to foster aspects of personal development: help children to relate to one another by playing 'Musical Hugs'. The children move freely around the room to music. When the music stops they find someone to hug. When the music starts they move off, this time as partners and join up with another pair to hug, until all the group are hugging one another. Help children to appreciate similarities and differences by playing 'This Is You, This Is Me' (best played in small groups). Give each child a mirror in which he or she views him or herself. Ask each individual to describe one of his or her features and compare this with that of their neighbour's. Share children's feelings by playing 'Tell Mr Rabbit'. A rabbit puppet wants to listen to what makes the children happy/worried/angry. The rabbit is passed round a circle of children in time to music. When the music stops, the child holding the rabbit says 'Mr Rabbit, I get sad when . . .'

- Help children to practise moral responsibility: encourage them to help, reassure and comfort other children in need and recognise this kind treatment publicly.
- Give time for silence and reflection: build quiet times into the daily programme. These might be explained as time for children 'to talk in their heads'; 'to think of beautiful things'; 'to be peaceful'; 'to listen to the sounds of the world'. Help children understand that silence is a gift to be enjoyed.
- Work in partnership with lunchtime assistants: these staff care for children at particularly important times of the day and need maximum support in their work. Try to ensure that your children have met their lunchtime assistant during one of the sessions prior to starting school; share with the assistant your approaches in fostering personal development and encourage the assistant to adopt similar attitudes and consistent ways of managing children; supply the assistant with a repertoire of games which will encourage co-operative behaviour; ensure that assistants have access to resources for children to use in the playground, e.g. skipping-ropes, balls, quoits, hoops.
- Show parents that they are valued: work closely with them in supporting their child's personal development; ensure that all parents receive at least one piece of 'good news' about their child during the first term in school.

Parents

- Consider how well you boost your child's self-esteem at home, e.g. through praise and physical affection; accommodating his or her mistakes; considering his or her worries and concerns seriously; taking time to listen and respecting his or her views; demonstrating

Suggested Action contd.
real interest in what your child does at school and in his or her social life.

• Provide a home environment to encourage social and moral development:

  – Encourage your child to practise self-discipline, e.g. to make choices and decisions about daily events and to solve problems for him or herself; children who are controlled with strict discipline do not know how to act when they are on their own.

  – Help your child to learn the consequences of his or her actions, e.g. if your child persistently takes biscuits out of the tin without permission and you continue to refill the tin without comment, he or she will not learn that these actions result in an empty tin with no biscuits for the rest of the family.

  – Make particular note when your child displays positive social attitudes, e.g. helping a friend, sharing toys, rather than concentrating on reprimanding negative behaviour.

• Use stories to help your child understand strong emotions and deal with difficult situations. The following are personal recommendations, but your local librarian should offer a more comprehensive list:

  – *Feelings/emotions*: Amos, J.L. *Feelings/emotions Series*, e.g. *I feel Angry, I feel Sad* (1990) Cherry Tree Press. These examine a range of emotions experienced by children in an amusing but reassuring manner.

  – *Death*: Perkings, G. and Morris, L. (1990) *Remembering Mum* (A. & C. Black, London). The boys' mum died and, with their dad, they made a special book about her.

  – *Hospitals/illness*: Reuter, E. (1989) *Christopher's Story* (Hutchinson, London). A sensitive account of how Christopher, his family and friends fight to conquer and so understand him contracting leukaemia.

  – *Divorce/separation*: Osborne, T. (1990) *Where has Daddy Gone?* (Mammoth, London). A sympathetic account of one little boy's experience of parent separation.

REFERENCES

1. Bolton, N. (1989) Developmental psychology and the early years curriculum,

in C. Desforges (ed.) *Early Childhood Education*. Scottish Academic Press, Edinburgh.

2. Coopersmith, S. (1968) Studies in self-esteem, in A. Cohen and L. Cohen (eds) *Early Education: The School Years*. Paul Chapman Publishing, London.

3. Conger, J.J. (1966) *Personality, Social Class and Delinquency*. Wiley, New York.

4. Haskey, J. (1983) Marital status before marriage and age at marriage: their influence on the chance of divorce, *Population Trends*, Vol. 32, pp. 4–14.

5. Hetherington, E.M. (1988) Family relations six years after divorce, in K. Pasley and M. Ihinger-Tallman (eds) *Remarriage and Step-Parenting: Current Research and Theory*. Guildford Press, New York.

6. Hetherington, E.M., Cox, M. and Cox, R. (1982) Effects of divorce on parents and children, in M. Lamb (ed.) *Nontraditional Families*. Lawrence Erlbaum Associates, Hillsdale, NJ.

7. Wallerstein, J.S. (1987) Children of divorce: report of a ten-year follow-up of early latency-age children, *American Journal of Orthopsychiatry*, Vol. 57, pp. 199–211.

8. Leach, P. (1994) *Children First*. Michael Joseph, London, p. 9.

9. Fountain, S. (1990) *Learning Together: Global Education 407*. Stanley Thornes, Cheltenham.

10. Barratt, G. (1989) A child's eye view of schooling, in G. Barratt (ed.) *Disaffection from School? The Early Years*. Falmer Press, Lewes.

11. Barratt, G. (1986) *Starting School: An Evaluation of the Experience*. AMMA, London.

12. Rogers, C. (1989) Early admission: early labelling, in C. Desforges (ed.) (1989) *op. cit.* (note 1).

13. Deci, E.L. and Ryan, R.M. (1985) *Intrinsic motivation and self-determination in Human Behaviour*. Plenum Press, New York.

14. Cooper, H. (1985) Models of teacher expectation communication, in J.B. Dusek (ed.) *Teacher Expectancies*. Lawrence Erlbaum Associates, London.

15. Donaldson, M. (1978) *Children's Minds*. Fontana, Glasgow, p. 117.

16. *Ibid.*

17. Lepper, M.R., Greene, D. and Nisbett, R.E. (1973) Undermining children's intrinsic interest with extrinsic rewards; a test of the 'over-justification' hypotheses, *Journal of Personality and Social Psychology*, Vol. 28, pp. 129–37.

18. Pepitone, E.A. (1980) *Children in Cooperation and Competition*. Lexington Books, Lexington, Mass., p. 23.

19. Barratt (1989) *op. cit.* (note 10).

20. Dixon, A. (1989) Deliver us from eagles, in Barratt (ed.) (1989) *op. cit.* (note 10).

21. Cooper, H. (1985) Models of teacher expectation communication, in J.B. Dusek (ed.) *Teacher Expectancies*. Lawrence Erlbaum Associates, London.

22. Ogilvy, C.M., Boath, E.H., Cheyne, W.M., Johoda, E. and Schaffer, H.R. (1990) Staff attitudes and perceptions in multicultural nursery schools, *Early Childhood Development and Care*, Vol. 64, pp. 1–13.

23. Wells, G. (1983) Talking with children: the complementary roles of parents and teachers, in M. Donaldson, R. Grieve and C. Pratt (eds) *Early Childhood Development and Education*. Basis Blackwell, Oxford, p. 37.

24. Nicholls, J.G. and Miller, A.T. (1984) Development and its discontents: the differentiation of the concept of ability, in J. Nicholls (ed.) *Advances in Motivation and Achievement: Vol. 3. The development of Achievement Motivation.* JAI Press, London.
25. Stipek, D.J. (1984) Young children's performance expectations: logical analysis or wishful thinking, in Nicholls and Miller (eds) (1984) *op. cit.* (note 24).
26. Rogers (1989) *op. cit.*, p. 105 (note 12).
27. Bruce, T. (1987) *Early Childhood Education.* Hodder & Stoughton, Sevenoaks.
28. Wood, V. (1989) School ethos and the individual within a community, in Barratt (ed.) (1989) *op. cit.* (note 10).
29. Willes, M. (1983) *Children into Pupils.* Routledge & Kegan Paul, London.
30. *Ibid.*
31. DfE (1994) *The Education Act.* Central Office for Information, London, section 156.
32. DES (1978) *Special Educational Needs* (the Warnock Report). HMSO, London, section 4.33.
33. Langois, J.H. and Downs, A.C. (1980) Mothers, fathers and peers as socialization agents of sex-typed play behaviours in young children. *Child Development*, Vol. 51, pp. 1217–47.
34. Morgan, V. and Dunn, S. (1990) Management strategies and gender differences in nursery and infant classrooms. *Research in Education*, no. 44, pp. 82–91.
35. Aboud, F. (1988) *Children and Prejudice.* Basil Blackwell, Oxford.
36. Goodman, M.E. (1964) *Race Awareness in Young Children.* Collier-Macmillan, London.
37. Jeffcote, R. (1979) Positive image, writers and readers, pp. 13–14, quoted in Menter, I. They're too young to notice: *Young Children and Racism*, Ch. 7. in Barrett (ed.) *op. cit.* (note 3).
38. Davie, C.J., Hutt, S.J., Vincent, E. and Mason, M. (1984) *The Young Child at Home.* NFER/Nelson, Slough.
39. Gammage, P. (1990) The social world of the young child, in C. Desforges (ed.) *Early Childhood Education (British Journal of Educational Psychology Monograph Series* no. 4). Scottish Academic Press, Edinburgh, p. 90.
40. Winick, M.P. and Winick, C. (1979) *The Television Experience: What Children See.* Sage, Beverly Hills, Calif.
41. Greenfield, P.M. (1984) *Mind and Media: The Effects of Television, Video Games and Computers.* Fontana, Aylesbury.
42. Dowling, M. (1989) Unpublished course material arising from a DES short course, Lincoln.
43. Greenfield (1984) *op. cit.* (note 41).
44. OFSTED (1994) *Handbook for Inspection of Schools: Guidance.* OFSTED, London, section 3.
45. Smith, P.K. and Cowie, H. (1991) *Understanding Children's Development.* Basil Blackwell, Oxford, p. 193.
46. *Ibid.*, p. 195.
47. Field, T. (1984) quoted in Smith and Cowie (1991) *op. cit.* (note 45), p. 102.
48. Parker, J.G. and Asher, S.R. (1987) Peer relations and later personal adjustment: are low accepted children at risk? *Psychological Bulletin*, Vol. 102, pp. 357–89.

49. Vaughan, B.E. and Langois, J.H. (1983) Physical attractiveness as a correlate of peer status and social competence in pre-school children. *Developmental Psychology*, Vol. 191, pp. 561–7.
50. Hallinan, M.T. (1981) Recent advances in sociometry, in S.R. Asher and J.M. Gottman (eds) *The Development of Children's Friendships*. Cambridge University Press.
51. Rubin, Z. (1983) The skills of friendship, in M. Donaldson (ed.) *Early Childhood Development and Education*. Basil Blackwell, Oxford.
52. Thomas, A., Chess, S. and Birch, H. (1970) The origins of personality, in D. Fontana (ed.) *The Education of the Young Child*. Open Books, London, p. 110.
53. Scarlett, W.G. (1983) Social isolation from age-mates among nursery school children, in Donaldson (ed.) (1983) *op. cit.*
54. Rubin, Z. (1983) The skills of friendships, in Donaldson (ed.) (1983) *op. cit.* (note 51).
55. Chapman, A.J. and Foot, H.C. (eds) (1976) *Its a Funny Thing Humour*. Pergamon Press, Oxford.
56. Athey, C. (1990) *Extending Thought in Young Children: A Parent–Teacher Partnership*. Paul Chapman Publishing, London.
57. McGee, P. and Chapman, A. (1980) *Children's Humour*. Wiley, New York.
58. Bruce, T. (1991) *Time to Play in Early Childhood Education*. Hodder & Stoughton, Sevenoaks.
59. Ziv, A. (1981) The influence of humorous atmosphere on divergent thinking, *Contemporary Education Psychology*, Vol. 8, pp. 68–75.
60. Nutbrown, C. (1993) *Threads of Thinking*. Paul Chapman Publishing, London.
61. Hamers, J.F. and Blanc, M.H. (1989) *Bilinguality and Bilingualism*. Cambridge University Press.
62. Raths, L.E., Harmin, M. and Simon, S.B. (1978) *Values and Teaching* (a *How to Teach It* book). Charles E. Merrill, Columbus, OH.
63. Piaget, J. (1932/1977) *The Moral Judgement of the Child*. Penguin Books, Harmondsworth.
64. Smith and Cowie (1991) *op. cit.* (note 45).
65. Singer, D. and Singer, J. (1990) *The House of Make-Believe*. Harvard University Press, Cambridge, Mass., p. 152.

4

YOUNG CHILDREN LEARNING

It is admittedly artificial to try to separate the child's personal and intellectual development as the two are closely linked. As we have seen, a sound base for learning is only established when the child is secure and confident. Early years teachers have traditionally been recognised for the high-quality care that they offer to children. Perhaps less evident to lay persons though, is the role they play in fostering the child's thinking and learning. In this chapter we consider the developments in understanding about young children's abilities to think and look – particularly at some key factors that support progress in learning.

It is now generally accepted that the young child entering school is a powerful, sophisticated and persistent thinker. Evidence for these findings have been made possible by a different approach to the study of young children's behaviour. In the past the usual way of checking abilities was to place the child in a controlled situation, involving new materials or experiences. The information received was heavily weighted towards what the child was not yet able to achieve. Piaget's study of the three-sided mountain was a classic example of this. Children were presented with a 3D model of three mountains and were asked to demonstrate, through using photographs, the perspective of a doll which occupied viewing positions different from their own. Clearly a daunting task, and not surprisingly beyond the abilities of most of the children. This led Piaget and Inhelder to state that the typical 4- or 5-year-old 'appears to be rooted in his own viewpoint in the narrowest and most restrictive fashion so that he cannot imagine any perspective but his own'.[1] The emphasis today is on observing the child in a more familiar situation and interpreting what he or she makes of it. The home is regarded as a particularly valuable context in which we can see children operating in a relaxed and confident manner.

Given this setting, even very young children can learn much that was thought to be beyond them. Dowling and Dauncey give an example of a grandmother with her 2-year-old grandchild. The adult points to the bookcase, nods her head and says to the child, 'Fetch me the dictionary please, Rachel'. Rachel assesses the situation, looks from her grandmother to the bookcase and puts her hand on a book. Her grandmother then shakes her head and the child selects another book. At this the adult smiles and says 'Thank you'. Rachel does not know what 'dictionary' means. However she selects one successfully because she understands the task, interprets successfully her grandmother's gestures and reacts to her affirmation.[2] These two examples demonstrate children being placed in very different learning situations. The first presents the child with significant obstacles which prevent the child from demonstrating what he or she might know. The second supports the child with a recognisable context and a number of clues all of which aid her success.

Some research studies have contrasted the constraints of a school setting which might limit the child's learning (particularly where there is an unfavourable adult–child ratio) with the opportunities offered in the home which may offer support, particularly in talk. MacLure and French concluded that the school setting may offer the child a more limited set of conversational options than he or she has become accustomed to in the home. While children are questioned and their spoken language is corrected both in school and at home, the study found that, while the child might question and correct the parent at home, it was rare to find the teacher having this reciprocal relationship with a child in a reception class.[3] Tizard's studies also indicate that children's speech at home is likely to be richer than that used in a day nursery or nursery school.[4,5]

As we have seen, most homes offer a young child an enabling background for development linked to a known and familiar setting and people. Schools cannot and should not try to emulate this. However, despite somewhat gloomy findings about schools failing to foster language, the child's first teacher is in a potentially strong position to develop the young mind. This position of strength is linked to the receptive nature of the young brain and the way in which young children regard their teacher as a model for learning. They want to learn and to please. The teacher's success in providing the appropriate degree of challenge in learning activities is heavily dependent on the teacher recognising the child's degree of competence. In order to do this it is essential for teachers to try to gauge some of the ways in which children operate mentally by the time they start school.

We turn now to some characteristics of thinking adopted by these young children which we can see through their patterns of behaviour, the language they use and the ways in which they become aware of their own approaches to learning.

SELF-DIRECTED LEARNING

Children do learn by their own efforts. They do not wait to be told about the world but use what resources they have to create scenarios and to predict circumstances. They are not dependent on adults overseeing their efforts or offering them extrinsic rewards. Instead, faced with a problem, they will attempt to solve it and even work towards improvement, having successfully achieved their initial goal. Children also progress in learning in this way. Karmiloff-Smith describes a group of children aged 4–7 attempting to construct a continuous railway circuit for a toy train, using both straight and curved segments of railway line. There is a clear sequence in the way the children attempted the task. The youngest children worked at random and, when the pieces did not fit together, they attempted to make them by the use of brute force. The second stage is that of local correction, when children removed the last piece of the track and adjusted it but ignored the rest of the construction. Third, children started again from scratch, even though parts of the assembly were correct and could have remained. Finally, the oldest and more mature children viewed the construction as a whole and made necessary adjustments to achieve success.[6] When this study was repeated, some of the children were determined to improve on this. Having built the system successfully, they dismantled it and built a new version, pointing out that there were several possible designs.[7] These two studies suggest that children progress from using trial and error, and partial correction, to being able to view the totality of the problem. They were learning from their mistakes and from successes and showed a sensitivity to alternative solutions.

SCHEMA

Chris Athey's research offers strong evidence for children's self-directed thinking strengthening through certain patterns of behaviour or schemes. She claims that children as young as 2 years become aware of features in their environment and develop related interests which they incorporate into repeated behaviour. Certain patterns or schemes are commonly noted during the years before school. Athey described these according to their physical features as follows:

- Dynamic vertical (up and down movements).
- Dynamic back and forth/side to side.
- Dynamic circular.
- Going over and under.
- Going round a boundary.
- Going through a boundary.
- Encompassing and containing space.

Athey argues that a child may become absorbed with one or more of these movement patterns and may represent it through action, through talk and through paintings and drawings.[8] Craig at 12 months repeatedly spilt his food on to the tray of his high chair and traced up-and-down lines in the liquid. When he started at toddler club he drew mainly vertical lines when finger painting. Later at nursery school, Craig was aware of the tall trees surrounding the building. His mother had discussed this with him and had taken a photograph of Craig standing by the side of one of the trees. Craig observed that, in the photograph, 'here is my head but you can't see the head of the tree'. Craig drew a number of pictures – that is, a series of vertical lines to represent symbolically the trees. In the reception class Craig initially spent a great deal of time practising his own 'writing', which was largely composed of vertical marks of a broadly standard size. In physical education and in discussion sessions, he demonstrated a good understanding of positional language, particularly 'up and down' and 'taller and shorter'. This small boy was also interested in other aspects of life, but here we see how one of his early patterns of behaviour persisted and was strengthened to support further learning.

Children may work on more than one schema at any one time. As they mature they begin to make connections between schema which in turn leads to new thinking. Nutbrown gives the example of a child's progress in drawing a human figure. She suggests that the child's early vertical marks are followed by oval representations and these in turn become linked together with horizontal lines to represent a person.[9] This progress is matched in symbolic play, block constructions and talk. However, children's schemes will only develop if they are fed with appropriate experiences.

CAUSE, EFFECT AND FUNCTION

As schemas develop children begin to make links in their learning. They investigate what causes something to happen and why. Four-year-old Richard discovered that, when he made big efforts to throw his ball, it went further than when he wasn't really trying. He had found that the distance of a ball depends on the power of the throw. In discussion with their teacher, a group of 4-year-olds came to understand that high and low notes are functionally dependent on the position of the teacher's fingers on a guitar fretboard. A young child needs to have a secure understanding of cause and effect as a precursor to understanding about conservation and that some materials, such as clay and sand, are capable of being reversed.

EMBEDDED TO DISEMBEDDED THINKING

We must accept that formal and abstract learning is not accessible for young children. This type of learning may involve theoretical situations or understanding and manipulating symbols. Margaret Donaldson suggests that this type of learning is disembedded from familiar and concrete situations. In this situation young children will fail.[10]

However, if we offer young children opportunities to think or problems to solve which are linked to known situations, or to familiar stories, they become significantly more competent. The learning has been placed in a human setting and makes sense to the child. If a 3-year-old is asked to divide 9 by 3, he or she is unlikely to succeed. If the same child is given nine cakes and asked to share them fairly among three dolls, the chance of him or her making sense of this request and performing competently is much greater. Margaret Donaldson would describe the former request as being outside or removed from the immediate concern of the child and using words in isolation. In contrast, the latter request is embedded in the child's current activity, the words have meaning within the context of play and the mathematical calculation is made possible for the child to demonstrate through a familiar action of giving and giving 'fairly'.

Two important requirements for children in school are to be able to concentrate and remember things. Woods suggests that the ability to focus on a task and ignore distractions is related to maturity and intellectual development.[11] Older children are able to use certain strategies, such as rehearsal and organisation, to help them concentrate and remember. The first involves rehearsing, or constantly repeating something to be learnt in order to hold it in one's mind. Organisation refers to the ability to order or structure items which in turn makes it easier to commit them to memory. Wood suggests that even when young children are shown these aids to learning and can appreciate their success, they will not automatically use them at a later stage. Wood also stresses the importance of embedded activities. Young children will not attend and remember things just because they are required to. However, their powers of concentration and memory are very evident in daily events that they find of interest. For instance, they quickly learn the layout of their classroom and their drawings and paintings often represent impressive and accurate detail of known places and people.

Most 4-year-olds will still be at the stage of thinking and talking about their own immediate concrete concerns. This is termed 'present moment embedding'. The next stage of thinking is still related to personal experiences but requires the child to recall the past and to project into the future. It is referred to as 'own-life embedding' and involves memories, plans and predictions that mean something to the child. However, as the child moves on in his or her educational career, the child will be required to tackle more formal and abstract thinking which is disembedded or removed from these personal experiences. Donaldson says that 'the better you are at tackling problems without having to be sustained by human sense, the more likely you are to succeed in our educational system, the more you will be approved of and loaded with prizes'.[12] That's putting it rather starkly, but it is vital that the most able children in the reception class begin to move towards thinking and solving problems which are not directly concerned with their own lives.

SOCIALLY INFLUENCED LEARNING

One major source of embedded experiences is linked to the child's interactions with other people. Development in thinking is heavily influenced by the child's participation in the social world. These beliefs, which have developed within the last ten years, have caused researchers to look carefully at the social setting of some of the test situations Piaget used. Margaret Donaldson and others concluded that, if children were able to make sense of problems posed to them, they were more likely to achieve success. Thus, when the 'three-sided mountain experiment' was subsequently adapted to allow children to express their understandings appropriately and within a familiar situation, many 4-year-olds 'clued in' to the test and provided a correct answer. Instead of using photographs to demonstrate an alternative perspective of the mountain, Borke asked children to demonstrate the doll's view by turning the mountain around, which was now mounted on a turntable. He then further modified the test by continuing to use the turntable but substituting animals and people in home settings instead of the mountain. This setting was presumably more like home than Piaget's Swiss Alps and thus less remote from the child's understanding and resulted in even more children achieving success. [13]

Children are therefore considered to be better placed to demonstrate what they know if a problem or test situation is placed in a familiar social setting.

However, more recently, the importance of social context has been reconsidered to have an even more central position in learning. Vygotsky's work supports the notion that mental processes start from the social behaviour and exchanges between people, and are then internalised to become part of the individual's thinking. Language exchanges are regarded as particularly significant in communicating meanings which a child can then use as the basis for his or her own thinking. This view of development means that discussions and social interactions are not only helpful but also critical in supporting the development of abstract thought. [14]

Vygotsky's findings support the value of collaborative work with young children. Following this thinking, Azmitia observed 5-year-olds working in pairs and produced the following conclusions. Having a partner can increase the amount of time children work on a task. The presence of a partner can prevent children from giving up in a difficult situation and it can also provide added enjoyment to the activity. Moreover, when children work together this can often increase their total work strategies: different children will bring different skills to a task. Finally, when less mature or able children are paired with an older or more able partner, the 'novice' learns a great deal from observing his or her partner and through benefiting from 'expert' guidance. [15]

SCRIPTS

One way in which children learn to place their world into an intelligible framework is by using 'generalised event representations' or 'social scripts' to describe everyday events. Nelson asserts that children as young as 3 years are able to organise their thinking in this way. Fivush gives an example of a 5-year-old child providing a script of her school routine after only one day in school:

> I just go to school/Then we do stuff. And then we have lunch or snack and then we go home . . . We play a little and then we go to the gym sometimes, or else we can go to the playground. And then we have snack, and then, in an hour, we have lunch. And then we can draw a picture or read and then we go home.[16]

Scripts are similar to schema in the way they support the child's thinking: they differ from schema by linking actions over a period of time. Within each script there are a series of events – the script of the child's school day consist of travelling to school, eating, working and playing. The detail included in each of these events will vary with the child's experience and age. However, scripts will typically involve a sequence of scenes which help children to recall activities, places and relationships and place them in a frame of reference. This in turn helps the child to feel in control of what he or she experiences. For instance, by developing a clear script from daily school activities, the child is able actively to predict the pattern of the day rather than be a passive recipient. Other significant findings related to scripts indicate that where children are particularly interested in events they tend to represent them in greater detail, and where they are familiar with an activity the represented script becomes more consistent and secure.

When using a script to recall events, most 4-year-olds are capable of using quite complex language, indicating some understanding of cause and effect, hypothesising (if . . . then) and time relationships (then, before, after, first). Teachers will be only too aware that many children of this age are not able to use this type of language in other daily classroom encounters. It appears that, by asking a child to describe a familiar personal experience, the child is supported by a secure framework for talk. Scripts also provide a structure for language, although studies indicate that this structure varies. Some events, such as going to a restaurant, involve a logical sequence of activities which must be followed in order to eat a meal. In contrast, an event such as a birthday party is more loosely structured and activities are not so clearly dependent on one another. A clearly structured event offers more support than one where the child is required to make decisions about the order of events in order to represent them accurately.[17]

However, a script does not have to have been experienced at first hand. Children develop social scripts in their role play and will learn scripts through vicarious experience of stories. All these opportunities offer a very positive context to enable children to demonstrate their understandings through language. Although good stories will offer children material for their scripts, children's own story-telling abilities at 4 years are likely to be relatively undeveloped. A script is a timeless account recounted in the first person, whilst a story is told in the past tense, provides specific characters, presents a problem and its solution and is likely to have a formal means of starting and ending. The ability to move from one to the other is a process of maturation.

METACOGNITION

Recent studies show that even very young children show signs of awareness of their own thinking. This awareness involves a person being able to monitor and adjust aspects of his or her learning and behaviour. It means having some understanding of how the person is performing a task, beginning to appraise what he or she is good at and where the person needs help. Clearly this type of self-knowledge and analysis is very necessary for mature learners. However, there is an early awareness demonstrated by children as young as 2 years. Meadows and Cashdan describe how at this age children are likely to become distressed if asked to tackle a task which they know is beyond their abilities: children younger than this will not show the same reluctance, by which we assume that they are not inhibited by knowledge of their own limitations.[18] Other studies have shown that preschool children are aware of the relation between their competence and that of others. In one study this was revealed by children deliberately choosing to observe a more expert partner at work on a Lego construction rather than to participate.[19]

Metacognitive activity is very much to do with a child becoming critically aware of what he or she is doing and being able to correct his or her own mistakes. Although part of the activity requires that specific skills and competencies are learnt such as holding a pencil and reading from the top of a page, children also need to gain an overview of their learning activities. If a child is not aware of the purpose and structure of a task, he or she may become 'bogged down' with learning subskills without being able to see their relevance. As children become more able to recognise and regulate aspects of their learning, they cease to be so reliant on the teacher and move towards intellectual independence.

Although it appears that some early awareness of thinking is present from a young age, Meadows and Cashdan suggest that children will only bother to learn to use and develop these metacognitive strategies if they are convinced that it is worth while.[20]

In summary, then, we find children at 4 years actively seeking to make sense of their world, being strongly influenced by social contacts and discussions with others, and becoming aware of aspects of their own thinking and learning. According to their level of maturation and the quality of their preschool experiences, individual children will be further ahead or delayed in their thinking processes.

The first year in school offers each child an opportunity to strengthen and extend his or her thinking, to use language as a tool for learning and to move towards understanding and using symbols and abstract thought. This growth and development is heavily reliant on the child's teacher and the teaching assistant, and we now consider the action that they must take under the broad headings of providing a context for learning, observing, managing learning, scaffolding and working with others.

Teachers can only decide how to develop children's learning by being clear what it is they already know. We have already considered how well children work when they are making decisions about their own activity: it follows, then, that self-directed activity is a profitable context in which children will reveal their thoughts and abilities. We now look at what this means in terms of classroom activity.

PROVIDING A CONTEXT FOR SELF-DIRECTED LEARNING

Although there is general agreement that young children will learn best through activity, the degree of self-direction involved remains open to debate. Polarised views about free play versus goal-directed structure are not helpful. Play continues to have an influential place in the early years curriculum: studies stress the value of play in demonstrating what children know. Spontaneous play allows children to practise and re-present knowledge which is already assimilated.[21] However, studies of classrooms suggest that many teachers are unclear about play's educational purpose – they offer it as a fringe benefit for children and as a gesture to the early years tradition. This invariably means impoverished provision, with the adult role relegated to occasional oversight of the activity and low-level responses from the children.[22]

However, increasingly reception teachers now recognise that self-directed activity for children implies scope for the child's enterprise but also allows a place for adult guidance and, when appropriate, adult involvement and intervention. This is not a compromise nor a dilution of the notion of self-direction, but is a recipe for the best learning processes and outcomes. As Tina Bruce suggests, 'At times the adult leads and at times the child. Each takes note of and responds to the other's actions and words'.[23]

Self-directed activity is often linked to the provision of play. In Bennett and Kell's study of activities with 4-year-olds, most of the activities were selected by the teacher, with the exception of play.[24] However, although play provides a rich context for children to select, make decisions and solve problems, it is necessary to consider all the other areas of provision where degrees of choice and decision-making might be included. This immediately widens the field. Self-directed activity described as above can be seen as an educational method which can be used as a vehicle for offering curriculum content in all areas of experience.

Two important points remain. First, the success of this method depends on real investment in self-directed activity which will allow outcomes of quality. Second, while acknowledging the central place of self-directed activity, teachers will recognise that it forms only one aspect of classroom practice. Children do learn in other ways, as we shall see. Moreover, the practicalities of a large class mean that the teacher can only properly provide for some children for some of the time to be engaged in pursuits where the main aim is for them to select and direct for themselves. However, many other activities will offer some scope for this way of working.

What then constitutes investment? Self-directed activity is no different from any other aspect of the curriculum in that it requires careful planning, good resourcing, adult time and ongoing monitoring and evaluation of the outcomes.

Teachers must have planned intentions for children as they are professionally responsible for ensuring progress in learning. However, planning does not preclude flexibility. Plans are based on the teacher's understanding of what the child can do now and what the next step in learning should be. The route for progression will also be planned but, within that, it should be possible to respond to the child's interests and strengthen the learning by taking account of what the child brings to it. Good planning therefore implies clear overall expectations. Within these limits there may be many opportunities for the child to select activities and make choices about methods to use. However, opportunities for choice and independence do not automatically lead to quality learning. Bennett and Kell paint a dispiriting picture of 4-year-olds being allowed freedom of choice and often opting for unchallenging activities. The examples of activities given are described as lacking purpose, structure and with no clear demand for process, product or challenge.[25] To counter this, though, other studies identify factors which support child-selected activity. The NFER study suggests that in the best practice there is nothing haphazard about allowing choice.[26]

The adult's planning can help to reduce a random and *ad hoc* response from the child. Planning needs to take account of teacher-initiated activities within which the child can make decisions, and also to prepare and allow the child to take a full degree of self-responsibility when he or she plans for him or herself. This latter way of working has been and remains traditional practice in many nursery establishments but has more recently been adopted in some mainstream classes under the High Scope programme.[27] Working in this way, the child is encouraged to project a plan of his or her activity for part of a session, to follow it through and to share some of the outcomes individually with the adult or within a small group. Within this plan–do–review approach, the adult can monitor the development of the children's abilities to plan and to follow their plan. Given the opportunity, children will also move from simply 'remembering' certain aspects of their actions to a more coherent recall, and move then to reflect and evaluate the outcomes. The Froebel Blockplay Project is rightly critical of adults requiring all children to state their work plans in advance, on the grounds that some individuals have their own internal plan which unfold in the 'doing': the ideas they wish to express are apparent in the process and product of the construction.[28] It is certainly important to recognise personal approaches to learning, and due respect should be given to those children who demonstrate their thinking in a non-verbal form. However, it is also in children's interests that they are guided towards securing their thinking through language, which may include projection and prediction as well as review.

The type and quality of self-directed activity is influenced by the accommodation and resources provided. For instance, Gura reports that, given a limited space in a classroom for blockbuilding, children worked in pairs on three-dimensional constructions. However, when they were able to take the blocks into the playground the children worked in larger groups and worked on horizontal grids, such as road and rail layouts.[29] Similarly, an inadequate supply of blocks immediately reduces the child's options for demonstrating his or her capabilities in planning and construction. If the environment is planned for self-directed activity, the space will allow for children to see what is available to support their learning and to have easy access to it. The High Scope programme suggests that the classroom should be divided up into well defined work areas and the materials in each area be logically organised and labelled. In the Froebel Block Play Project, Gura suggests that 'the care and concern and presentation of blocks are all ways of indicating that we adults value this activity'. She also emphasises that high-quality outcomes of block play are a process of interaction between maturation and environment.[30] Thus a well resourced and a spacious and accessible area provided for an activity such as block play allows children to explore and work with materials in depth, which in turn means that they make strides in learning.

The pattern of the school day has already been discussed in Chapter 2. However, it is worth reiterating that, when planning the overall daily programme, teachers will be aware of the need for children to have opportunities for blocks of time to get involved, develop and perhaps complete their activity. If the activity is ongoing or complex, as in some imaginative or construction play, children need time to realise what they have achieved and to experience satisfaction. Stephenson reports that, given the opportunity, children will spend long periods of time at a self-chosen activity.[31] However, Gura urges caution in taking duration of time as a strong single measure of concentration. She quotes an example of a child confidently completing a block representation of an owl in less than two minutes and suggests that this is simply the outcome of considerable previous background knowledge of birds and of mastery gained over blocks. Consequently, it is only by noting what children do with their time over a duration that it becomes possible to judge the quality of time spent on one activity.[32]

Teachers know only too well how their time and attention can enhance the value of children's activity. They are also faced with the dilemma of dealing with large numbers of children who have different needs according to temperament and their stage of learning development. Early years specialists who contributed to the NFER study on 4-year-olds advocated a flexible timetable with the minimum of interruption to the day. This allows children the blocks of time for sustained activity but also gives the teacher opportunity to target his or her time with individuals and small groups. This targeted time is precious and merits very clear thinking about how it is to be used.

OBSERVING

If a good learning context of self-directed play is offered, it provides the teacher with many opportunities to observe children in action and, in particular, to note their schemes of thinking. These will be revealed through their talk, actions, models, drawings and paintings. The categories of schemas outlined earlier in the chapter will provide a useful framework for observation. Cathy Nutbrown suggests that, by using these categories, it helps to make sense of activity which otherwise might appear a series of disconnected events. Nutbrown describes children's schemes beautifully as 'threads of thought' which sometimes link their actions across different subject content.[33] A 4-year-old may, given the choice, engage in a number of apparently disconnected activities. He or she may persist in making 'hidey holes' in fantasy play, spend time on a representational painting and then obliterate it, use clay or dough to 'cover' beads or bricks, and when sticking and making he or she repeatedly makes 'parcels' to give to the teacher or to friends. If the teacher simply observes from the perspective of content, these actions look random and disconnected. However, viewed in terms of the child's thread of thought, there is the clear link of enveloping and containing space. By observing children in this way teachers can gain valuable insights into children's current interests and forms of thinking and thus form a positive view of their capabilities.

These observations can also help teachers in their planning. Nutbrown points out that, when considering continuity of learning for young children, the response is usually to plan through topics or themes which link together various subjects or areas of experience. Such topics can have very worthwhile features, including relevant and interesting activity, which draw on the child's experience. However, Nutbrown suggests that this is essentially the offered curriculum planned by the teacher. In order to identify what children have learnt, it is necessary to study the links they have made in their learning which may be revealed through schema.[34] Having recognised children's schema it is possible to offer further curriculum content to strengthen the child's existing interest and build on his or her current understanding. Chris Athey suggests that the early years curriculum could be more effective if it were planned on the basis of children's interests as opposed to the teacher arbitrarily deciding on a topic heading.[35]

MANAGING LEARNING

So far we have concentrated on activities that are predominantly child initiated. In reception classes there is also an important place for teacher-led activity, particularly where these involve early literacy and numeracy skills. In these cases it is important to ensure that children are given an experience which helps to develop their learning. We draw on the work of Bennett and Kell and look at learning management under some of the headings they use, namely, teacher intentions, presentation, match and task implementation. (The assessment aspects of the teacher's role is discussed in Chapter 7.)

HMI report that 'The advent of the National Curriculum has thrown many issues concerning provision for the reception class into sharp relief'. One of these issues is planning or teacher intention: although HMI report that the quality of planning in the schools was very mixed, they write that 'at best there was an excellent framework for sequencing the work and indicating how it would be taught and managed'.[36] This is a marked improvement when compared with their report four years previously, where the majority of primary classes with 4-years-olds were described as having 'little evidence of teachers' systematic planning for the introduction and development of knowledge, concepts and skills through investigation, imaginative play, the use of natural materials or construction'.[37]

However, Bennett and Kell were more concerned about the teacher's planning intentions not being made clear to the child. They quoted cases of teachers' instructions for tasks being inaccurate and inadequate. One example was of the teacher planning for the child to acquire number recognition of 1–5 through counting and recognition or numbers of farm animals. Yet the activity was suggested to the child in terms of 'Would you like to play with the farm?' Consequently, no counting took place and there was no requirement for it.[38] In this case the child had no idea of what was expected of her and the teacher made no attempt to check that her intentions were being implemented. In other cases the teacher may be more specific, but the messages are not being received. Margaret Donaldson suggests that a young child may be seen to fail to carry out a task or to respond to an instruction, not because he or she is incapable of that task, but because the child cannot comprehend the adult's use of language.[39]

Providing a task which is pitched at an appropriate level of difficulty for each child is a formidable job for any teacher, and particularly daunting for the reception teacher with a new intake. Bennett points out that across age levels of children from 5 to 15, there is evidence of teachers underestimating their high attainers and overestimating their low-attaining children. In the 4-year-old study the findings are similar, although the quality of matching was observed to vary widely from teacher to teacher.[40] In a smaller study, Sestini had previously reported similar problems with achieving a match of task for this age-group when the activity was teacher directed.[41] Clearly, a well matched task is dependent on an accurate assessment and consequent diagnosis for the next step in learning (see Chapter 6).

Bennett and Kell rightly point out that, even where a task is well planned, clearly presented and pitched at an appropriate level, it can come to nothing at the implementation stage. Children need to be motivated, to concentrate and apply their previously acquired knowledge to the task. Poor implementation may be linked to poor classroom conditions which spring from unsatisfactory class management and basic class control.[42] In his sociological study of infant classrooms, Ronald King emphasised that the teachers who were most satisfied with their classroom control made their expectations and rules for work and behaviour quite explicit and used approval and praise when these expectations and rules were kept.[43]

The major implication here, then, is for teachers to ensure that children know what they are doing and why they are doing it. The other requirement for successful implementation is to ensure that the child is equipped for the learning and has sufficient support for the task in hand.

SCAFFOLDING

Current thinking and recent research stress the value of the teacher's direct role in promoting learning. This teaching role will take different forms and will be shared by paid and voluntary teaching assistants.

There are many approaches to teaching: our concern here is using the most effective mode for young children. Wood's work with mothers and trainers on 'instructional styles' used with 4- and 5-year-olds explored the following ways of working:

Level 1   Adult uses general verbal encouragement.
Level 2   Adult uses specific verbal instruction.
Level 3   Adult assists in choice of material.
Level 4   Adult prepares material for assembly.
Level 5   Adult demonstrates an operation.

Wood points out that, at levels 4 and 5, the instruction is at its most intensive while, at the same time, the child's responsibility for the task is diminished. His study concluded that, where mainly demonstration was used, children learnt little. The most effective instruction proved to be a combination of levels 1, 2 and 3, that is, of showing and telling. The adult works alongside the child providing sufficient to help but not to undermine.[44]

Wood's work supports both Vygotsky and Bruner, who state that the child as a relatively inexperienced learner will learn a great deal from the adult as one more experienced. Vygotsky suggests that we should see the child as being at two levels of development. The first is the present level and reflects what the child is able to do unaided. The second level is identified by the teacher as what the child could do with some guidance and support from a more knowledgeable person. The gap between these two levels is termed by Vygotsky the 'zone of proximinal development'.[45] Thus the teacher's time should be spent with children working within this zone. The teacher's aim is to move children from a position of dependence to achieve tasks independently at a new and higher level of development.

Bruner describes the adult's role as 'scaffolding'. Initially the scaffolding may involve offering considerable help and this is reduced as the child becomes more competent and confident. Successful scaffolding requires the teacher to make a sound judgement of what the child knows now, an accurate diagnosis of the next learning step and appropriate support to enable the child to achieve it. Wood suggests that 'Four-year-olds can be taught to do tasks that, alone, they will not master until around age seven or eight. For them to learn, however, instruction must be geared to that (changing) level of competence. When this condition can be and is achieved, young children can be taught and do learn'.[46]

The teacher will scaffold in different ways according to his or her knowledge of individual needs. Although each child requires particular support with his or her learning, scaffolding can take place within the context of a group. The teacher will use some of the following strategies.

Play tutoring

While most children entering the reception class are likely to have had experience of imaginative play, a minority may be inexperienced. In his study of socially isolated children, Scarlett found that these children were less likely to become involved in imaginative play.[47] It may be that these children need active help in learning to play symbolically. Smilansky and Freyburg found that children who received such assistance made noticeable gains in their play. Smilansky termed this process 'pump-priming'. If the child is not active in an imaginative setting, she suggests that the teacher plays and reacts as if the child were role playing.[48] The teacher might say, 'Oh good morning, I think that you are the new doctor, aren't you? I have come to see you because I have this pain in my arm. I wonder if you would examine it for me?'

A similar type of support can be offered through storying. Freyburg played with a small group of children using pipe-cleaner dolls and other improvised materials. She worked with the children to act out prepared stories. When these children were compared with a control group they were found to have improved their powers of imagination and concentration.[49]

The teacher will want to identify those children who need play tutoring. However, he or she may delegate the work to a teaching assistant who would be in a position to give ongoing support until the child is capable of 'holding his or her own' in a group.

Conversing and questioning

While the teacher's role in play tutoring is specific to some children, his or her role in promoting talk, although easier with some children, is important to all. The teacher's aim should be to enable all children to share their feelings, thoughts, ideas and attitudes.

The effectiveness of adult–child conversation both at home and at school is well researched. Wood explores how adults can help children converse with them freely and openly. His transcripts of many child–adult conversations reveal that the adult who offers his or her personal views, ideas and observations tends to receive many of the child's views. This leads to a genuine sharing of experience. Conversely, the adult who controls the conversation and who asks questions persistently may receive minimal answers but rarely elaborations or opinions. The conversation thus becomes dominated by the teacher.[50]

It is clearly essential for teachers to gain access into children's minds by encouraging them to talk freely and openly. However, sensitive questioning will help to clarify and extend children's thinking. Mercer describes how teachers elicit information from children in order to check what they already know. He suggests that much of this work is through offering cues and clues in order to lead the child to the 'right answer'.[51] This strategy is useful if it is used as a means of scaffolding the child's own understandings. However, when over-used simply to ensure that the teacher's goals are met, it merely creates an image of learning.

The predominant message from research is that nursery and reception classrooms provide insufficient opportunities for dialogue which promotes children's thinking.[52] HMI stress that good standards of literacy are achieved where the development of spoken English is taken seriously through story-telling, discussion and effective questioning. They report that in half of the schools in the reception class survey these aspects were underemphasised.[53]

However, a marked contrast is reported in KS1 classes which were observed at a similar time. HMI report that English at KS1 offers a heartening picture. The inspectorate found that the good standards from the previous year had improved further:

> it was largely due to teachers' confident and judicious use of questioning and discussion. When teachers organised small groups of pupils for the discussion of clearly defined matters, when they listened carefully to pupils, and when they required pupils to answer questions which were carefully posed, standards were high. A particularly effective focus for the development of talking and listening was story telling.[54]

I cannot accept that work in reception classes is so different from that in years 1 and 2, and can only assume that in reality there is still a wide variety of practice in operation. Moreover, however well intentioned, the teacher with a large class of young children always encounters considerable difficulties in making time for this work. David Wood's findings point clearly to the need to talk with children individually and in small groups. This can only be helped by realistic adult–child ratios and careful planning of the total adult time that is available.

Encouraging use of narrative

One important outcome of dialogue is to allow children to provide narrative accounts of their activities, in which they will reveal through their 'scripts' – their ability to sequence and make sense of the event. A traditional occasion for this has been provided through 'news time', when children gather as a group and are invited by their teacher to share items of interest with their peers. This occasion needs to be skilfully handled. At worst, 'news time' can result in a heavily teacher-dominated session in which too few children are actively involved: the constraints of time and the formality of the occasion restrict narrative accounts from most individuals to brief and low-level headlines. The rest of the class are required to listen passively to accounts which do not necessarily directly involve or interest them. However, this practice can be adapted to provide the maximum opportunity for children to demonstrate, strengthen and enhance their scripts. This may be through

- using known stories where children can predict what comes next and weave alternative content into familiar scripts;
- adults and children planning activity for a session and subsequently reviewing what has been achieved;
- conversation sessions using practical activities in small tutorial groups; in this way a teacher or teaching assistant can offer more time for each child to contribute, could encourage elaboration of scripts and could foster more shared discussion;
- identifying scripts used in role play; the adult can act as a play tutor and encourage the child to recount the script of actions of the character he or she is playing; and
- the teacher keeping a running record, particularly on the scripts of new children in order to monitor their language development.

Moving from first-hand to abstract thought

As mentioned previously, when young children are locked into embedded thinking this is rooted in tangible and concrete experience from which they are unable to generalise. In order to move them on to abstract disembedded thinking, the teacher must essentially move into the child's mind and help him or her to make links in the child's learning. There is need to offer interesting content as a vehicle for learning. It's salutary to note John Brierley's caution that, when a child is faced with learning that does not involve him or her, it leaves no trace of any experience on the child's brain networks.[55] Conversely, if we offer young children access to relevant and rich experience that, in itself, stimulates the desire for further inquiry. With young children as with adults, the more they know the more they want to know. By encouraging all forms of representation of these experiences, including symbolic play, drawing, painting, constructing and talking, the teacher is allowing the child to distance him or herself from the immediate context. This is the first move towards helping them generalise their understandings. The teacher will, moreover, help to crystallise these understandings by scaffolding these representations through prompting, questioning and offering practical help.

However, the intention is not to move children away completely from embedded thinking. Both adults and children need opportunities to strengthen abstract thought by referring back to particular concrete situations. Blenkin describes the teacher's aim as helping the child to build bridges between concrete experiences and abstract thinking.[56]

Aiding metacognition

In helping children to become more aware of their thinking, the teacher needs to give them full information about his or her intentions for their learning. When children are introduced to the purpose and structure of a task, they are better able to see the reason for tackling component parts. As we saw, the teachers in Bennett and Kell's study did not score well on this.

Children also need to be introduced to component parts of their thinking, such as planning, memorising, concentrating and reviewing, to discuss and refine these learning strategies and then helped to apply them deliberately. The teacher will also encourage self-criticism and evaluation. Even 4-year-olds can be helped to see their strengths and limitations. The clearer the child becomes about his or her capabilities as a learner, the better equipped he or she is to use them deliberately in future learning. Meadows and Cashdan suggest that 'thinking about your thinking' seems to be an effective way of getting better at it, and also to be a source of self-confidence.[57]

WORKING WITH PARENTS

There are now numerous studies which stress the powerful role that parents can play in their child's learning and development. Two of these include Tizard *et. al.*'s study of children in 33 London infant schools, which found that the strongest predictor of attainment at age 7 was the amount of '3Rs' knowledge the children had before they started school.[58] The HMI survey on reading standards identified parental involvement as one of the main criteria to be found in those schools with good standards of reading.[59]

Despite this, as we saw earlier, it appears that some parents do not recognise the potential of their role (see Chapter 1). Moreover, some teachers continue to be sceptical of the preparedness of parents to take on such a role and participate actively in their child's learning. In the Tizard *et. al.* study 29 per cent of the infant teachers interviewed predicted that none or very few of their parents would wish to help their child once the child had started school. A further 16 per cent felt unable to suggest whether there would be any involvement. However, this view from the teachers contrasted strongly with the parents' expressed intentions. With very few exceptions, the 202 parents interviewed said that they would want to continue to help their child at home once he or she had started school.[60] Two nursery studies by Hannon and James reveal similar pessimism from teachers, which are not supported in practice. The first study showed that not only were parents interested in helping to develop literacy skills but also that they were already involved in many reading and writing activities with their children. Although not linked to this study, Hannon and James again found some of the headteachers from the nurseries involved expressing doubts about parents having such interests and commitment.[61]

Apart from perceiving a lack of motivation, some teachers have concerns about parents not having the correct approach to educating their children. In the Tizard *et. al.* study, one in four of the reception teachers said that they disapproved of parents teaching any reading, writing or number to children under the age of 5; those who said that they approved were anxious that nothing was taught that would be incompatible with what was taught in school.[62] Hannon and James stated that the nursery teachers in their study believed that parental involvement in developing literacy skills could result in children being placed under too much pressure and being taught by wrong methods.

Despite having these anxieties, the teachers in both of these studies only offered limited advice as to what assistance parents could give their children. In the Tizard *et. al.* study the onus was on parents to ask for assistance.

This rather negative picture of teacher attitudes and actions is counter-balanced by my observations of innovative and effective teacher/parent links in schools. However, it is imperative that practitioners explore, honestly acknowledge and share their beliefs about working with parents. Low expectations of parents as with children will lead to self-fulfilling prophecies.

Although some teachers merely pay lip service to the work, perhaps because of genuine reservations, others have a real commitment to learning from what parents know of their children. This latter group aim to develop a shared expertise into gaining insights into the young child's mind. The Froebel Early Education Project achieved this impressively. Parents and teachers worked together as joint learners, investigating children's schema and fostering the development of schema both at home and in the nursery school. Parents know a great deal about their children but are understandably often hazy about the processes of learning which take place. They can remember the subject-based, exam-orientated curriculum which they experienced, and this is easier to understand than the early years curriculum. However, it is important that parents do come to an understanding in order to protect this curriculum. Joyce Watts argues that, 'if the child-centred curriculum is to survive within National Curriculum guidelines, then not only must teachers be seen to be committed to it, but parents must identify with it'.[63] Moreover, when teachers take time to explain to parents the significance of what children do and how this has value for learning, the children will derive benefits. When parents are able to interpret their child's behaviour, they are better able to support it. This develops into an upward spiral of success as inevitably the child's symbolic experiences will be enriched and the parent is able to recognise his or her central role in achieving this. Athey summarises this: 'nothing gets under a parent's skin more quickly and more permanently than illumination of his or her own child's behaviour'.[64]

CONTINUITY

We are looking at the first phase of education as part of a continuum. The opportunities offered to children, the skills and concepts developed and the working links made with parents in the reception class should ideally be sustained when children move into the next class. The considerable amount of work that has occurred in promoting continuity of practice between classes has until now been more focused on curriculum content. In particular, teachers have concentrated on making links with practice in the reception class and National Curriculum attainment targets and levels of attainment. However, if continuity of learning is to become a reality it requires teachers to consider together how the child functions as a learner. This includes shared understanding of the child's cognitive learning style – how he or she approaches learning – as well as the strategies the child employs and the stage he or she has reached in representing understandings. The inclusion of parents in these discussions will add a further dimension of information about the child. It will also powerfully demonstrate the principle of partnership to parents; help the receiving teacher have an intimate knowledge of the child as a learner; and be a most effective springboard in enabling the child to progress. Although this practice of collaboration is beneficial for all families, in reality of course it is very time consuming and may only occur in regard to those children whose learning processes are particularly difficult to track or who cause concern.

Finally, this chapter turns full circle, because all planning and interventions will come to nothing unless the teacher believes in his or her children. We have already indicated how teachers' expectations of individuals can very rapidly become self-fulfilling. Mortimore *et. al.*'s study of junior-age children shows how teachers can communicate low expectations whilst having the best intentions for the children. For example, Mortimore *et al.*'s observations of classrooms revealed that children regarded of lower ability tended to have more contacts with their teacher and to receive more feedback than those deemed more able. However, the nature of the feedback differed in that the 'lower ability children' received more comments about their behaviour and were praised for their work. By contrast, teachers used their time with more able children to discuss and develop their work. The research team concluded that it appeared that teachers were prepared to be less critical of the less able individuals and simply to offer encouragement for whatever was achieved. However, they also suggested that these junior-age children might deduce hidden messages from the ways in which they were treated. 'The real meaning of such praise may be that the performance is poor, or the expectations are lower'.[65]

Although 4-year-olds' achievements may not be immediately affected by teacher expectations (see Chapter 3), the Mortimore report confirms that these expectations very soon have a powerful effect on individuals. Mortimore *et al.* emphasise that 'The responsibility of teachers is to ensure that their pupils do not adopt fixed views of their own abilities but rather, come to realise that they have considerable potential, which given motivation and good teaching in an effective school can be realised'.[66] The reception teacher plays a particularly important role in setting the tone.

Suggested action

Headteacher

- Organise meetings with new parents and preschool group workers entitled 'Ways in which your children learn'. Present different methods. Introduce a workshop activity which enables parents practically to experience the effectiveness of exploration and application as educational methods.
- Foster whole-school awareness of metacognitive processes and chart the ways in which characteristics are developed in different age-groups, e.g. reflection, self-monitoring, overview of task.
- Agree a whole-school policy and practise for promoting continuity and progression in learning; provide opportunities for teachers to observe the children they will receive in their current class; stress the need for teachers to share documentation and discuss individual children's learning processes.

Governors

- Request that your reception teacher runs a governors' training day on 'Young children learning'.
- The parent governor can liaise with parents in order to find out if they have sufficient information about how their children are learning. Note and report areas of confusion and misconceptions as well as those practices which are valued.

Preschool groups

- Use the information about children learning gained at school meetings as a tool for evaluating your preschool provision, e.g. given the physical constraints of your setting, what choices are children allowed to make?
- Ensure that children have time to explore fully such materials as

---

blocks, paint, sand and water in order to provide a good base-line for extension in the reception class.

- Observe and note the schematic concerns of your oldest children. These notes can be shared with parents and with the receiving teacher.

Teachers and teaching assistants

- Plan for self-directed activity: help children to use the environment. Aim to provide a self-service resource area; allow time initially for children to familiarise themselves with the materials through exploration in each of the areas. Help children to make choices when planning: provide books of photographs of the different activities in the classroom; use this as an *aide-mémoire* which serves to remind individuals what is available. Help children plan: recognise that children are at different stages in being able to plan; some individuals will find it difficult to project their intentions and may simply offer a headline which defines the activity; the significance of the learning may be revealed if the plan develops in detail and scope during the implementation. Help children to gain knowledge and skills in use of materials: note the child's current level of knowledge and skill, e.g. able to apply adhesive, able to mix paints. Build on this by demonstrating new skills in small-group times, e.g. a sequence for mixing paints using brush, powder paint to palette, brush to clean water; by recognising a child's new achievement and incidentally drawing it to the attention of others, e.g. the ability to create right angles using blocks; by encouraging children to share new skills with others in 'sharing time', e.g. 'David, will you show us just how you made your print so clearly?'; by allowing children to observe one another and so gather information to expand their own plans.
- Enrich and extend thinking: provide routines, activities and out-ings which are discussed and compared, allowing children to strengthen their event scripts. Provide links between embedded and disembedded thought. Help children to generalise, e.g. use the story of *The Three Bears* to gain a concept of '3'. Introduce a different word each week, e.g. 'teacher'. Encourage children to share concrete examples of their understanding of the word. Help children to decentre by using stories and discussion which help them explore other viewpoints, e.g. 'How did each of the three

Suggested Action contd.
little pigs feel when the wolf visited? How did the wolf feel?'
- Nurture metacognition: help children to be aware of the learning processes that they need for a task, e.g. 'Now when making up our own story of the gingerbread man, we must try to remember the story in the book, we must share our thoughts for some new adventures for the gingerbread man, and we must agree about an exciting ending for the story'. Use questions which encourage reflection and self-criticism, e.g. 'That's an interesting painting, Emile. Are you pleased with it? What bit do you like best? Tell me more about it. Do you think that this is your very best work?'

Teachers and parents

- Help parents to be aware of the power of their child's learning: run workshops on children's learning which summarise the main activities which have occurred during the past half term and outline the main strands in children's progress. These can be demonstrated through annotated displays of work or records of responses in activities and on outings which exemplify children's thinking. Offer information about schema to parents prior to their children coming to school; this may be discussed during home visits (using a photograph album of graphical examples) or at a group meeting (using slides of examples). Parents can be encouraged to observe their child's mental schemes at home and to share these observations with the teacher when the child is admitted. The form of observation can vary from a detailed written diary to some shared comments with the teacher. Promote a partnership to support the child learning: keep a home–school schema notebook going. Parents, teachers and teaching assistants can contribute any significant change or development in the child's interest and way of recording it. The notebook can be used at parent–teacher consultations. Where some model of High Scope curriculum is used, encourage parents to share in the planning of their child's daily programme. Keep a planning book for each child in which he or she is helped to think through and record selected activities and intentions for the session. Suggest that parents discuss these plans with their child and scribe them at the beginning of each session. The plans will be used later by the teacher when monitoring activities and in group reflection and review. Listen very carefully to what parents are saying about their child; their observations and comments are likely to reflect a knowledgeable and intimate picture, which will offer an important extra dimension for you as a professional.

- Link with receiving teachers: although some liaison is likely to be ongoing throughout the year, the following practice focuses on facilitating the child's learning when he or she transfers to the next class. Aim for two planned meetings between the reception and year-1 teacher, and three half-day visits for the year-1 teacher to visit the reception class. The initial meeting is used to share schema notebooks, records and individual observations of children. During the three visits, the year-1 teacher can use this information and target his or her observations on different children. These observations will be shared with the reception teacher, together with discussion about programmes for individual children.

REFERENCES

1. Piaget, J. and Inhelder, B. (1956) *The Child's Conception of Space*. Routledge & Kegan Paul, London, p. 242.
2. Dowling, M. and Dauncey, E. (1984) *Teaching and Learning 3–9*. Ward Lock, London, p. 21.
3. MacLure, M. and French, P. (1981) A comparison of talk at home and at school, in G. Wells (ed.) *Learning through Interaction*. Cambridge University Press.
4. Tizard, B. (1979) Language at home and at school, in C.B. Cazdan (ed.) *Language and Early Childhood Education*. US National Association for Young Children, Washington, DC.
5. Tizard, B. and Hughes, M. (1984) *Young Children Learning*. Fontana, London.
6. Karmiloff-Smith, A. (1979) Problem solving construction and representations of closed railway circuits, *Archives of Psychology*, Vol. 47, pp. 37–59.
7. Deloache, J.S. and Brown, A.L. (1987) The early emergence of planning skills in children, in J. Bruner and H. Haste (eds) *Making Sense*. Methuen, London.
8. Athey, C. (1990) *Extending Thought in Young Children: A Parent–Teacher Partnership*. Paul Chapman Publishing, London.
9. Nutbrown, C. (1994) *Threads of Thinking*. Paul Chapman Publishing, London.
10. Donaldson, M. (1978) *Children's Minds*. Fontana, Glasgow.
11. Wood, D. (1988) *How Children Think and Learn*. Basil Blackwell, Oxford.
12. Donaldson (1978) *op. cit.* (note 10), p. 113.
13. Borke, H. (1983) Piaget's mountains revisited: changes in the egocentric

landscape, in M. Donaldson (ed.) *Early Childhood Development and Education.* Basil Blackwell, Oxford.

14. Wood, D. (1980) Teaching the young child: some relationships between social interaction, language and thought, in D. Olson (ed.) *The Social Foundations of Language and Thought.* Norton, New York.
15. Azmitia, M. (1988) Peer interaction and problem solving: when are two heads better than one? *Child Development,* Vol. 59, pp. 87–96.
16. Fivush, R. (1984) Learning about school: the development of kindergarteners' schools scripts, *Child Development,* Vol. 55, pp. 1697–709.
17. *Ibid.*
18. Meadows, S. and Cashdan, A. (1988) *Helping Children Learn.* David Fulton, London.
19. Azmitia (1988) *op. cit.* (note 15).
20. Meadows and Cashdan (1988) *op. cit.* (note 18).
21. Hutt, C. (1971) Exploration and play in children, in R.E. Herron and B. Sutton-Smith (eds) *Child's Play.* Wiley, Chichester.
22. Meadows and Cashdan (1988) *op. cit.* (note 18).
23. Bruce, T. (1987) *Early Childhood Education.* Hodder & Stoughton, Sevenoaks, p. 23.
24. Bennett, N. and Kell, J. (1989) *A Good Start? Four Year Olds in Infant Schools.* Basil Blackwell, Oxford.
25. *Ibid.*
26. Cleave, S. and Brown, S. (1991) *Early to School: Four Year Olds in Infant Classes.* NFER/Nelson, Slough.
27. Hohmann, M., Banet, B. and Weikart, D. (1979) *Young Children in Action.* High Scope Press, Ypsilanti, Mich.
28. Gura, P. (ed.), with the Froebel Blockplay Research Group, directed by Tina Bruce (1992) *Exploring Learning: Young Children and Blockplay.* Paul Chapman Publishing, London.
29. *Ibid.*
30. *Ibid.,* p. 163.
31. Stephenson, C. (1987) The young four year old in nursery and infant classes: challenges and constraints, in *Four Year Olds in School: Policy and Practice.* NFER/SCDC, Slough.
32. Gura (ed.) (1992) *op. cit.* (note 28).
33. Nutbrown (1994) *op. cit.* (note 9).
34. *Ibid.*
35. Athey (1990) *op. cit.* (note 8).
36. OFSTED (1993) *First Class: The Standards and Quality of Education in Reception Classes.* HMSO, London, p. 13, para 31.
37. DES (1989) *Aspects of Primary Education: The Education of Children Under Five.* HMSO, London.
38. Bennett and Kell (1988) *op. cit.* (note 24).
39. Donaldson (1978) *op. cit.* (note 24).
40. Bennett and Kell (1988) *op. cit.* (note 24).
41. Sestini, E. (1987) The quality of learning experiences of four-year-olds in nursery and infant classes, in *Four-Year-Olds in School: Policy and Practice.* NFER/SCDC, Slough.

42. Bennett and Kell (1988) *op. cit.* (note 24).
43. King, R. (1978) *All Things Bright and Beautiful.* Wiley, Chichester.
44. Wood (1988) *op. cit.* (note 11).
45. Vygotsky, L.S. (1986) *Thought and Language* (revised and edited by A. Kozolin). MIT Press, Cambridge, Mass.
46. Wood (1988) *op. cit.* (note 11), p. 81.
47. Scarlett, W.G. (1983) Social isolation from age mates among nursery school children, in Donaldson (ed.) (1983) *op. cit.* (note 13).
48. Smilansky, S. (1968) *The Effects of Sociodramatic Play on Disadvantaged Children.* Wiley, Chichester.
49. Freyburg, J.T. (1973) Increasing the imaginative play of urban disadvantaged kindergarten children through systematic training, in J.L. Singer (ed.) *The Child's World of Make Believe.* Academic Press, London.
50. Wood, D. (1992) Teaching talk, in K. Norman (ed.) *Thinking Voices: The Work of the National Curriculum Project.* Hodder & Stoughton for the National Curriculum Council, London.
51. Mercer, N. (1994) Language in educational practice, in J. Bourne (ed.) *Thinking Through Primary Practice.* Routledge/The Open University, London.
52. Meadows and Cashdan (1988) *op. cit.* (note 18); Tizard and Hughes (1984) *op. cit.* (note 5).
53. OFSTED (1993) *op. cit.* (note 36).
54. OFSTED (1993) *English Key Stages 1, 2, 3 and 4, 1992–3*, para 2, p. 6. HMSO, London.
55. Brierley, J. (1984) *A Human Birthright: Giving the Young Brain a Chance.* British Association for Early Childhood Education, London.
56. Blenkin, G.M. and Kelly, A.V. (eds) (1987) *Early Childhood Education: A Developmental Curriculum.* Paul Chapman Publishing, London.
57. Meadows and Cashdan (1988) *op. cit.* (note 18), p. 56.
58. Tizard, B., Blatchford, P., Burke, J., Farquar, C. and Plewis, I. (1988) *Young Children at School in the Inner City.* Lawrence Erlbaum Associates, Hove and London.
59. HMI (1990) *The Teaching and Learning of Reading in Primary Schools.* DES, London, p. 2.
60. Tizard *et al.* (1988) *op. cit.* (note 58).
61. Hannon, P. and James, S. (1990) Parents' and teachers' perspectives on pre-school literacy development, *British Educational Research Journal*, Vol. 16, no. 3, pp. 259–71.
62. Tizard *et al.* (1988) *op. cit.* (note 58).
63. Watt, J. (1990) *Early Education: The Current Debate.* Scottish Academic Press, Edinburgh, p. 130.
64. Athey (1990) *op. cit.* (note 8), p. 66.
65. Mortimore, P., Sammons, P., Stoll, L., Lewis, D. and Ecob, R. (1988) *School Matters: The Junior Years,* Paul Chapman Publishing, London, p. 170.
66. *Ibid.,* p. 264.

5

THE FOUNDATION CURRICULUM: PRINCIPLES AND PLANNING

CHARACTERISTICS OF YOUNG CHILDREN STARTING SCHOOL

This chapter will start with a recap of the personal and learning characteristics of young children when they start school. We see that the child's self-image has been heavily influenced by early family experiences and this in turn affects the way in which he or she views new experiences and trusts his or her own competence as a learner. Children arrive at school with a massive diversity of past experiences: from these experiences they have acquired attitudes and social dispositions which affect how they relate to other adults and children, the way in which they regard the world and come to understand the rules for living. At 4 and 5 years, children are remarkably well developed intellectually and are actively trying to make sense of all that is around them. Their understanding is only restricted because of their immaturity and limited experience of life. Thus they are able to think about and discuss their own personal concerns and activity, but are not yet able to apply learning from these experiences in an abstract way. Young children learn a great deal from other children and adults through observing and, sometimes, imitating them and through the sharing of ideas. When given the opportunity to learn actively and talk and interact with others, children will develop their own ways of developing their ideas which include schemes of behaviour and frameworks, or 'scripts' of social events. They also show signs of awareness of their own activity and thinking and an ability to adjust and correct their actions.

This summary emphasises how rapidly and effectively young children learn. We must also remember how strongly their self-esteem and general appetite for learning are affected if they do not feel recognised as a special person, if they do not understand what is happening in school or are not given opportunities to succeed. This in turn means careful attention to the curriculum that is planned and offered in the reception class. We will look at the broad principles which underlie the early years curriculum, the content that is offered and the way in which it should be offered.

CHARACTERISTICS OF AN EARLY YEARS CURRICULUM

Children of all ages, of course, require a curriculum which is based on meeting their needs. However, young children particularly require a curriculum that is concerned with them because, for many, it will be their first experience of learning in an educational setting. If so, the early years curriculum is their first encounter with planned opportunities to promote their learning. Unless this curriculum touches them, these opportunities are not realised, the child's powerful social and learning dispositions are not developed and the overall effect is negative rather than positive to future learning.

Educationalists past and present who are concerned with young children recognise the need for a curriculum which aims to keep in touch and respond to children. It includes the following characteristics:

- Recognition of the children's previous learning experience and the building of new learning based on what has previously been learnt.
- Provision of interesting and varied active and first-hand experiences which motivate the child to learn.
- A broad range of opportunities which allow children to represent their understandings of what has been experienced.
- A cohesive and unified approach which acknowledges and promotes all aspects of children's development and supports links in their learning.
- A social context in which children share their learning with one another and with other adults.
- Provision for children to make choices and decisions as part of helping them to be in control of their learning.
- Links into the beginnings of the KS1 curriculum.

THE EDUCATIONAL CLIMATE AND THE CURRICULUM
FOR YOUNG CHILDREN

The main argument in this chapter is that the curriculum must match with the child's needs and stage of development. Many would argue strongly that current educational policies and statutes prevent this happening, and that some Victorian attitudes (such as utilitarianism, uniformity and discipline) indicate that we are moving into an era of 'hard' control as opposed to 'soft' control of education.[1] Whitehead suggests that the delivery and receptive modes of teaching and learning are dominant: 'Children are taken to be empty vessels, unmoulded clay, or recalcitrant recruits to the human race who must be licked into shape and fitted for society'.[2]

There has been, and still is, understandable anxiety about the appropriateness of the National Curriculum (NC) for young children. For instance, Blenkin and Kelly suggest that the NC is not concerned with children learning, but more to do with subject content that has to be assimilated; that it is focused on product rather than process and that the model of planning is instrumental through aims and objectives; and that progression and continuity is stressed in terms of structure of subjects, rather than what is known about children's development.[3] Other fears relate to the imposition of the NC on younger children: 'this downward pressure to teach a diluted form of content and knowledge . . . ignores the view of education as a subtle and sophisticated process of development which must be based and planned at every stage by reference to intrinsic principles rather than extrinsic aims'.[4]

These points are well made and I share a number of them. Moreover, the authors rightly express views which reflect the demoralisation of some early years practitioners who feel that their work with young children has recently been marginalised and threatened as a result of pressure from a top-down and centralised curriculum.

Other concerns are related to the status and training of adults who plan and organise the curriculum for young children. Blenkin and Kelly point out that the lack of recognition of child development as a valid subject in initial teacher education must result in deprofessionalising teachers which, in turn, must reduce the quality of their provision:[5] 'Teachers do need to be clear-sighted about the political context of their work, and prepared to be assertive to gain better conditions. They need to be articulate, organised and skilful in acting as a voice for young children . . . They need to become political advocates on behalf of young children.'[6]

However, teachers also need encouragement and support to work with their children despite these perceived difficulties. It is in the spirit of lifting teacher morale and seeing just what is possible that the following points are made.

The first is to indicate that, despite the undisputed stresses of the pace of change and the problem of overcrowded content, not all teachers have felt undermined and pressurised by the NC. Observations of KS1 classrooms in 150 schools revealed different types of teacher response to educational reforms. These included

- *compliance* – accepting the change and getting on with it, which was predominantly the response from younger teachers;
- *retreatism* – involving demoralisation and alienation, and mainly a response from older teachers who were unable to adapt; and
- *mediation* – welcoming the changes and making creative uses of the statutory requirements.

Although the last group were in the minority, the authors of the study suggest that if change had been more sensitively introduced in collaboration with teachers, the 'mediators' might well have been the majority group.[7]

Second is the suggestion that some developments in recent years have raised the level of awareness about the need for good-quality provision for early years. The child's achievements in the statutory curriculum are increasingly seen to be dependent on what has happened to the child during the years before statutory schooling. In order to combat the danger of this being a demand for the NC to start earlier, the onus is on schools and educationalists to stress the appropriate content and methodology for these young children. Hurst provides a good example when she states firmly that 'it is possible that without the learning opportunities offered by play, the aims of the National Curriculum will not be achieved, since it is through play that learning becomes meaningful to children'.[8]

Additionally there has been some minor resourcing for early years classrooms. The quality of the curriculum is recognised as being dependent on the quality of the adults. Although the reasons for introducing increased support for the training of teaching assistants are politically suspect, the outcomes for young children are beneficial. The support amounts to tacit acceptance that the second adult in the classroom does much more than providing an extra pair of hands. There is long-standing acceptance that nursery classes will be staffed by a trained nursery assistant and the training of teaching assistants for work in primary schools is a move towards similar provision. HMI found that where NNEB-trained nursery assistants supported the teachers of the youngest children, this enabled teachers to provide work that was better matched to the developing abilities of the children, to organise group work more effectively and to give more attention to the needs of individuals. In short, the training of assistants should enhance curriculum opportunities for children.[9]

Finally, many of the real worries about the NC concern children at 6 and 7 years as they approach the end of KS1 assessments. Our focus is on younger children during their first year in school. It can be argued, of course, that the younger children are also affected if the demands on years 1 and 2 impose pressures on children in year R attaining certain standards. This is a danger, and some reception classes have succumbed by providing a curriculum which simply regards all children in year R, regardless of age and stage of development, as participants in the NC. However, these appear to be in a minority. HMI report that less than 10 per cent of reception teachers in their study felt under pressure from the school or parents to teach the NC. Moreover, most reception teachers in the survey had found the statutory orders and some of the non-statutory guidance useful as a reference for their own planning.[10] It is important to stress that applying the statutory curriculum to children in their foundational year does not meet the requirements of OFSTED, who at last make clear statements about the type of curriculum to be offered to children under 5. Even more importantly, even the revised statutory curriculum applied to all children when they enter school is counterproductive to raising the quality of learning or standards of achievement for many.

THE RECEPTION CLASS

Many reception-class teachers have been uncertain about their curriculum responsibility. Nursery teachers, although mindful of the need for continuity, are not bound by the NC. Teachers in other primary classes are at least clear about the stage of the NC to be taught within their year group. In most reception classes there are children of both 4 and 5 years of age. This has caused considerable confusion as to when the NC starts for these children.

The legal definition of compulsory school is the term following their fifth birthday. If children are admitted to school at the beginning of the autumn term during which term they will have their fifth birthday, for the duration of that term they are considered to be of non-statutory school age and for NC purposes they are described as pre-KS1.

In practice there is wide variation of when children are admitted to school although, as we have seen, there is a move towards one point of entry to start school in the autumn term. The DfE statistics for 1993 state that 56 per cent of 4-year-olds were admitted to reception classes during the autumn term, with a further 19 per cent admitted in the January. All these children were of non-statutory school age.[11]

Thus the number of children in a reception class who are of statutory school age and therefore thought subject to the NC will vary each term and throughout the year. In the spring and summer terms reception classes probably have more pupils who have reached statutory school age. The messages about these children have until recently been unclear. For the purposes of inspection, the decision as to whether the class is described and inspected against the NC has been founded on the age of the majority of the children in the class at that time. However, SCAA speak more clearly. They emphasise that their own planning group planned for KS1 over six terms and that there is no requirement in the new orders to teach NC subjects in the reception year.[12] Teachers can feel secure that the curriculum offered to the children in the foundation year should be a nursery-based programme which dovetails closely into the beginnings of the NC programmes of study. This curriculum provides a bridge from home, nursery and playgroup experience to the start of the NC.

Admittedly, the resources in a reception class in terms of accommodation, adults and equipment may not match those offered in a nursery class and, because of this, it will be more difficult to offer children the same opportunities for choice and spontaneous, self-directed learning. However, it should not be assumed that all 4-year-olds will have vastly diminished learning opportunities in mainstream school. Jenefer Joseph, in passionately defending the 4-year-old's right to nursery education, suggests that in a reception class one would expect to find a clear distinction between work and play: the daily programme dominated by the teacher rather than allowing for child-chosen activity and a lack of provision for play with sand and water.[13] This gloomy picture is not denied in some classes, but should be counterbalanced by the examples of good and imaginative practice described in the NFER study.[14] However, Cleave and Brown admit that this practice is not easily achieved. Given that so many of our 4-year-olds are in school, the important question to ask is why the quality of experience for some is so much better than for others.

Early years teachers are committed and want the best for their children. Some cannot realise this because of physical constraints, large classes and lack of teaching assistance. Others are unsure about what constitutes a curriculum for the reception class. The remainder of this chapter deals with the key elements of planning the reception-year curriculum.

PLANNING

Teachers must have planned intentions for children as they are professionally responsible for ensuring progress in learning. However, planning does not preclude flexibility. Indeed, careful planning will allow some detours to be made with confidence, because the teacher is secure in his or her knowledge of the path towards the next learning goal. It is possible to respond to the children's interest and adapt the planned route accordingly.

During recent years, early years teachers have spent thousands of hours developing their planning, and miles of paper have been used in recording planning formats. Good things have happened as a result, most noticeably the collaborative planning between teachers. However, having been through these time-consuming exercises many schools are now reviewing their planning, sometimes with the view as to how it can be pruned to be more effective. The following suggestion offers a possible framework for planning for the first year in school.

Long-term planning

A common approach by teachers to long-term planning is to start with planned intentions each year and then, on the basis of review at the end of each term, simply reallocate their time in the following term's plan. This actually ignores the fact of 'knock-on effect'. If plans are not realised each time, the cumulative effect of aspects of curriculum not dealt with over a period of years is considerable. Time is finite: the three terms allocated for the foundation year equate to approximately 798 hours. In order to use time most effectively to ensure a broad and balanced curriculum and to plan experiences for children which are in their best interests, some hard decisions must be made and priorities given to what is to be taught in this time.

Initial planning will be concerned with considering all that needs to be done with and for young children during their first year and then allocating and distributing time for these activities over the three terms. Although initially teachers may want to consider the allocation in terms of percentages of time, it is important that these percentages are translated into actual hours. By looking at actual time, teachers are forced to recognise that when planning a curriculum which is heavily dominated by literacy, mathematics and the physical area of learning, this effectively squeezes out areas of other learning.

Admittedly this exercise is not one which comes easily to early years teachers. They see it as a theoretical task, very much to do with timetabling and very little to do with children's learning. However, a serious study of how time is allocated is helpful in considering how it might be used better. Perhaps a more persuasive argument is that, to ensure that children do learn about art, music and technology, time must first be secured in order for this to happen. When looking at the relationship between the length of the taught week and the quality and standards of pupils' work, OFSTED conclude that an adequate amount of teaching time 'is a necessary but not sufficient condition for producing work of quality' . . .[15]

Having identified an amount of time to be allocated for a particular activity, over the year, decisions about how that time is distributed will be influenced by how the activity is best offered to children. Two main categories include, first, the activities that need to be offered regularly and frequently such as early literacy and number work; second, those activities which perhaps need to be offered within a defined period of time. Again, this is a difficult exercise for early years practitioners. Many would argue that all areas of learning need to be available to children daily. Certainly time needs to be allowed for child-selected activity, but a programme must ensure also that not only is a broad and balanced curriculum made available for children but that it is also experienced. Young children will not always choose to investigate everything that is on offer to them. Moreover, children also need to work in groups and to be taught skills and introduced to new ideas. Time for this work needs to be carefully planned. Finally, curriculum breadth must be planned in conjunction with opportunities for children to learn in some depth. In order to achieve this, the balance of the curriculum over a day needs to be considered against the balance for a week, a term and over the course of the year.

Once decisions are taken about the frequency of offering curriculum content, it is possible to see exactly what one term's worth of content in the reception class looks like. Further questions may then need to be asked about whether it is manageable both for the child and for the teacher and if it looks to be a well balanced and sufficiently broad curriculum diet. When the curriculum analysis has been decided and agreed within the school, ideally this framework should remain and be reviewed at the end of the year. However, a small amount of contingency time, say 5 per cent, will allow some flexibility for readjusting time allocations.

Medium-term planning

Once a framework of time has been established, decisions can be made about how the curriculum content will be organised. The two forms of curriculum organisation are through discrete teaching of aspects in an area of learning and through grouping areas of learning together into crosscurricular topics or themes. Much of the learning for young children will be organised through crosscurricular topics. Although reading, handwriting and aspects of mathematical learning will necessarily be taught separately, there will be further opportunities for children to apply their learning within practical topics. Certainly, topic work is an economic way of organising time and curriculum content; topics can also provide relevant and interesting contexts for learning. Teachers are increasingly realising that topics are most effective when they are selected as a vehicle for children to learn specific skills, concepts and attitudes within a limited focus rather than expecting them to service all areas of learning. The planning of topics can also exploit the natural links within and between the different areas, for example, between technological and mathematical areas of learning or human and scientific.

Short-term planning

If long-term planning is concerned with organisation of time and medium-term planning concentrates on organisation of content, weekly and daily plans are more concerned with the activities and methodology through which the curriculum is offered. Decisions will be made about the forms in which areas of learning are offered to children and the methods used, whether this is through storying, exposition, questioning or investigation. Topic work with 4-year-olds will clearly always be underpinned by opportunities for speaking, listening and play and, as we have already noted, these are the most effective methods for enabling young children to learn.

Short-term planning includes consideration given to the span of ability in the class and the ways in which the curriculum activities are to be differentiated. Plans will also consider both human and material resources. Curriculum opportunities for children should be enhanced on those occasions where there is additional teaching and voluntary assistance.

Teachers are also increasingly planning for outcomes. Unless there is clarity about what the children should be learning, it is not possible to know if the teaching has been successful. If planning is not linked to and does not affect what the children learn, it becomes simply an expression of hope and no more. To ensure that this link is ever present, planning must be based on clear judgements about what the children have already learnt and a view of what is to be learnt next.

Suggested action

Teachers and teaching assistants

- Long-term planning: include in your planning all the activities that have time implications in the reception class, including establishing routines and introducing children to new activities (helping children to become pupils); time for transitions (particularly at the beginning of the year); time for parental activities (parents-and-children workshops; parents helping their children plan at the beginning of the day); time for concerts or annual celebrations.
- Medium-term planning: when planning for discrete work, decide what needs to be taught regularly and frequently in order for children to progress in learning. When planning for topic work, decide on the areas of learning to include in your topic, and consider 1) how the links in one area of learning may provide a useful stimulus for work in another, e.g. literacy (Aesop's fable, The Stork and the Crow) with science (displacement of water); 2) how skills or concepts learnt in one area might be applied in another, e.g. mathematical (learning about pattern) with art; and 3) how common knowledge might be shared, e.g. technological (use of 'roamer' in planning routes) with mathematical.
- Short-term planning: work with Y1 teachers and list all the methods that you use to offer the curriculum to children; consider your reasons for using each method and how well you achieve a varied and balanced methodology.

Teachers and parents/governors

- Share your curriculum analysis: publish your long-term planning

---

> *Suggested Action contd.*
> (curriculum analysis) for the foundation year by including it in a booklet for new parents. This will help them to see clearly the curriculum their child will be offered each term.

REFERENCES

1. Whitehead, M. (1993) Why not Happiness? Reflections on Change and Conflict in early Childhood Education, in P. Gammage and J. Meighan (eds) *Early Childhood Education: Taking Stock*. Education Now Publishing Co-operative, Ticknall, Derbyshire, p. 1.
2. *Ibid.*, p. 3.
3. Blenkin, G.M. and Kelly, A.V. (1994) *The National Curriculum and Early Learning: An Evaluation*. Paul Chapman Publishing, London.
4. Wilson, J. (1994) Early years curriculum, *Forum*, Vol. 36, no. 2, p. 44.
5. Blenkin and Kelly (1994) *op. cit.* (note 3).
6. Pascal, C., quoted in Gammage and Meighan (eds) (1993) *op. cit.* (note 1), p. 19.
7. Pollard, A., Broadfoot, P., Cross, P., Osborn, M. and Abbott, D. (1994) *Changing English Primary Schools?* Cassell, London.
8. Hurst, V. (1991) *Planning for Early Learning: Education in the First Five Years*. Paul Chapman Publishing, London, p. 49.
9. DES (1992) *Non-Teaching Staff in Schools: A Review by HMI*. HMSO, London.
10 OFSTED (1993) *First Class: The Standards and Quality of Education in Reception Classes*. HMSO, London.
11. DfE (1994) *Pupils under Five Years of Age in Schools in England, January 1993. Statistical Bulletin, 6/94*. DfE, London.
12. SCAA (1995) Planning The Curriculum at Key Stages 1 and 2, pp. 617, SCAA, London.
13. Joseph, J. (1993) Four year olds in school, in Gammage and Meighan (eds) (1993) *op. cit.* (note 1), p. 15.
14. Cleave, S. and Brown, S. (1991) *Early to School: Four Year Olds in Infant Classes*. NFER/Nelson, Slough.
15. OFSTED (1994) *Taught Time: A Report on the Relationship between the Length of the Taught Week and the Quality and Standards of Pupils' Work including Examination Results*. OFSTED, London, p. 9.

6

THE FOUNDATION CURRICULUM: AREAS OF LEARNING

We now look at the types of experiences that will comprise the curriculum. The experiences leading to aspects of personal development and learning have already been discussed (see Chapter 3), but these should be central when planning for all areas of learning. The headings used are those suggested by OFSTED. Even though each area of learning links into the statutory curriculum subjects, the use of terminology which is different from the NC signifies that early years is a phase in its own right.

LINGUISTIC AND LITERACY AREA OF LEARNING

The four language modes of talking, listening, reading and writing should receive priority. Oracy has already been discussed in relation to children's learning (Chapter 4). Children's talk will underpin all subsequent achievements in written language and so will be the focus of work with new and younger children. Children should have daily opportunities to talk with adults and other children in a variety of groups and different settings. They will use language to describe their actions and past experiences, to ask questions and to project and hypothesise about future events. Imaginative play will provide a major context for talk. Reported tangible outcomes from fantasy play include approximately half the time during which children are talking spontaneously, an increase in social interaction and a noticeable increase in use of rich and complex language. These benefits may occur when children are left to their own devices. However, when the adult takes a part in the play using the children's ideas and language, the benefits are increased.[1]

Children have acquired a wealth of knowledge and experience in regard to reading and writing before they come to school. However, these experiences differ. HMI report that the socioeconomic background of the school was directly linked to the quality of the children's preschool literacy experiences. The inspectors also found a clear link between children coming to school well prepared for literacy and achieving high standards in reading and writing in the reception class.[2] The teacher's first task is to observe each child's attempts to read and record in a variety of different situations. The level of understanding may range from one or two children who are already able to read and write with some facility and enjoyment to those who have had very little experience of books or stories and who are not yet aware that text offers a message. Where play is planned to include explicit literacy experiences, it can offer children valuable opportunities to show and practise their competencies in reading and writing. Nigel Hall suggests that play, which is based on real-life experiences, allows children to

- encounter print in a meaningful way;
- experience literacy which is needed for the play rather than for isolated instruction;
- use literacy for their own purposes;
- use reading or writing skills separately or together as required in everyday life;
- learn about literacy from one another.[3]

Close collaboration with parents will provide the teacher with further insights into the child's understanding of print. Experts suggest that links with the family are particularly important in the case of bilingual children, where children may be becoming literate in more than one language. The teacher needs to be aware of the experiences in the first language that children will use when learning to read and write in English.[4] The ability to listen and remember what others have said is an important learning skill. However, young children will only listen if they are really interested in what is being offered. This is usually the case when listening to stories and rhymes. Stories told without using books enable children to listen to the pattern of language, focus on the story-teller's means of expression and understand another important use of oral communication.

Listening to stories linked with text is significantly associated with children's development as readers and writers. Young children need to be read to frequently, at least twice a day: if possible, more often for those children who have not had stories read to them at home. Children who are read to frequently are learning a great deal about how to read for themselves. They will see the pleasure and purpose of reading, come to experience a wide vocabulary and hear word and phrases that rarely occur in spoken language.

Don Holdaway considers how the stories that parents have shared with their children at bedtime are recalled by the child to be represented in play, and then used as a basis for the child's own reading. Holdaway suggests that this approach can be used systematically in school. The teacher can introduce a new text through a story, encourage children to familiarise themselves with it through the teacher re-reading it and through activities related to the text, and finally through independent experience and expression when children read, tell or role play the text for themselves.[5]

Children who have had many stories read to them will want to try to write their own. The teacher may act as group scribe for shared story writing or encourage children to retell their own stories through pictures and captions. When reading back their stories, children are supported by a known text.

Young readers and writers need to become aware of the similarities and differences in spoken words. Research indicates that phonological awareness (recognising that words can be split into sounds) develops through familiarity with nursery rhymes.[6] Children who have developed this listening skill are helped in making sound/symbol correspondences. Extensive experience of rhymes, songs and word games which involve rhyme and alliteration will help to strengthen children's knowledge of words as sounds. At the same time, children will become increasingly interested in deciphering print and noting letter/sound relationships. Their own names and the names of their friends will provide a starting point. The class environment that is richly resourced with displays of print will help children see how words are written. Early knowledge of the letters of the alphabet is necessary for children learning new words. It is helpful if they learn letter names initially: the letter sounds which are closely linked to the names will be learnt relatively easily. The new level descriptions and new programmes of study for reading reflect research findings on the use of rhyme and alliteration, and the importance of early letter-name knowledge in reading development.[7]

Many children are able to read words in everyday contexts even if they cannot read them in isolation. Outside visits can encourage children to read signs and slogans. They can bring from home different examples of packaging texts, including those written in different languages.

The teaching of links between letters and sounds will occur incidentally and through direct instruction in a phonic programme. However, children are not ready to learn about sounds in relation to symbols until they know the alphabet and have developed phonological awareness. Some children develop a knowledge of phonics simply through rich literary experiences which they have received before coming to school. Others will need to be taught this strategy, but only as appropriate to their needs and ensuring that they use it when reading early texts. The use of phonic cues is helpful for young readers and was recognised by HMI as a contributory factor in supporting good standards and quality in literacy. However, HMI stress that the young readers they observed were not over-reliant on phonics but employed other skills and read for meaning.[8]

As well as receiving group stories, children need the opportunity to share books with one another and to browse as individuals. These times will provide the adult with valuable insights into children's abilities to initiate and sustain a story, their book-handling skills and their book preferences. A reception class should include a well resourced and well used book area. Although there is no reference to reception classes, Meadows and Cashdan quote several studies of nursery classes and schools where the emphasis is focused on the provision rather than the use of provision.[9] More usually, children were given free access to use books; they visited the book area infrequently and briefly. It is important in nursery and reception classes that books are brought to the children's attention and made a focus for learning. This will involve planning for regular time in the programme.

Children will practise their reading skills throughout their time in school and at home. Their reading will include the interpretation of public print from labels and advertisements, reading for information, and reading narrative. The debate about the benefits of using 'real books' against 'scheme books' continues. Importantly, the child needs access to books of interest, which offer a wide experience of written language and support the reader to use all his or her strategies to make sense of the text. These criteria may be met through both types of book.

As with reading, HMI found that the child's early experiences heavily influenced his or her standard of writing in the reception class. The children with high standards of writing came to school knowing about the purposes of writing, most knew how to form and recognise some letters and were able to write their own names. They wrote freely in play activities and could match sounds and shapes of letters and words.[10] These children will only form part of the class: HMI also found individuals who had a very limited understanding of the conventions of writing. However, although children's early experiences of writing will differ, they are likely to arrive in school with a common motivation to write. Their subsequent success in writing is dependent on fuelling that enthusiasm by giving children the confidence and opportunity to write for themselves and supporting their development in writing. This is the core of the writing curriculum in the reception class.

It is important that the child's initial writing is unaided. He or she will have opportunities to write freely within play contexts, but the writing produced is incidental to the play. The teacher will also want to set up a purposeful writing activity when children are encouraged to think about their writing and how things are written and discuss this. Handwriting and spelling will not feature at this stage: the emphasis is on communication and clarity of the message.

In order for children to continue as confident writers, they need to have reasons and different audiences for writing, to try out their writing and to be able to share their writing with an adult. Hall's view that young children are authors involves the belief that they are capable of making decisions about what and how they write: 'A teacher who forces her children to copy or insists on taking control of the writing done by the children in her class can never know if the children can function as authors'.[11] Some classroom practitioners who support this notion of authorship offer strong evidence both of the quality of writing produced from young children and the children's positive attitudes engendered towards writing. The examples offered by these nursery and reception teachers include arranging for children to engage in written dialogue with a fantasy character, and exchanging letters and dialogue journals with the teacher. By setting up a classroom noticeboard one teacher enabled her 4- and 5-year-olds to produce a range of brief texts that conveyed messages about different aspects of their social and school life.[12]

Children will also need support with their writing. The teacher's role is concerned with establishing a writing environment, providing models of writing and helping to develop and improve their writing.

Apart from ensuring that role play is a source for writing, there is need for a well stocked writing area, a variety of print displayed in the classroom and a comfortable book area where models of different texts are available.

The children also need to see the teacher as an adult engaged in the process of writing. He or she will provide this by acting as a group recorder and scribing children's thoughts and views: by drawing children's attention to features of print in books and classroom displays; and through making explicit the teacher's own purposes for writing in the classroom, such as marking the register, writing notices for displays and keeping a personal diary.

The teacher will also work with children to develop and improve their writing. Initially, the teacher may ask children to consider what words look like or what letter words begin with. He or she may write the correct version of what the child has written underneath the child's text and help the child to compare the two versions. When the child is confident in attempting his or her own writing, the teacher will introduce spelling and handwriting. Both are important aspects of learning to write but are not the main core of writing.

Researchers suggest that children pass through the following stages in learning to spell. These comprise

- the preliterate stage when writing may resemble text but there is no evidence of any sound/symbol knowledge;
- the early phonemic stage when the child begins to use letter names to represent words, e.g. 'EC'(easy), 'R' (are); the phonetic stage when there is recognition that letters can represent sounds in words, e.g. *hospl* (hospital), *nis* (nice);
- the transitional stage when children become more aware of the visual aspects of words as well as how they sound; and
- the final stage when children use visual and word-building strategies which include knowledge about letter names, letter sounds and letter strings to produce mainly correct spellings.[13]

Other studies indicate that children's early word inventions help them gain some understanding of the rules of spelling. Moreover, until children are able to produce their own invented spellings, they are unlikely to be helped to spell correctly.[14]

The main aims of teaching handwriting should be to help children to write legibly, easily and with reasonable speed. Learning to form letters correctly is not easy for young children: however, as they become comfortable with the physical process of writing, they are more able to free their thoughts for composition. As they learn to write legibly, they are able to communicate in print.

As with other aspects of writing, the teacher's role is to provide appropriate materials and to instruct children how to form letters. The concern that cursive writing may be required for attainment by year 2 has now, thankfully, disappeared. Teachers are now able to look at the more essential question of whether to learn joined-up script from the start is compatible with children's development. Sassoon's suggestion to introduce children from the beginning to exit strokes appears a sensible compromise.[15] Whitehead suggests that 'just as good reading teachers encourage and support children who begin to read silently, no matter how young they are, so this research appears to recommend support for children who move to a flowing cursive at an early stage.[16]

Suggested action

Preschool groups

- Plan times when children share books with adults individually or in very small groups: use these times to note how children handle books and their book preferences.
- Use a core of rhymes and songs which stress matching word sounds; play special guessing games with small groups of children, e.g. ask them to listen for the word that makes the same sound as 'frog'; whoever identifies it, chooses the next rhyme.

Teachers and teaching assistants

- Build reasons for reading and writing into activities and daily routines, e.g. provide named stickers or pens and stickers for children to label their work in construction and painting areas; allow children to register themselves on entry to school by identifying their name card and placing it on a display board; provide a noticeboard which the teacher and children can use to communicate messages: these can be shared orally once a week.
- Establish literacy role-play areas: provide a wide range of play contexts which involve reasons for being readers and writers, e.g. a travel agent can be resourced with timetables, brochures, posters, forms, tickets, telephone and notepad.
- Decide on a core of approximately 20 books that you will use as

Suggested Action contd.
a basis for promoting early literacy with your children; purchase several copies including large formats of these books. Use these texts for story-telling; instructing in the conventions of print; allowing children to 'read' the texts for themselves at school and at home and to read to others; encouraging children to write their own stories.

Teachers and parents

• Have a planned strategy for welcoming and encouraging parents to share their child's literacy development with the school. Provide information, e.g. details of local library services during term and holiday times; a simple guide on how to exploit children's reading skills when visiting the supermarket. Develop a literacy diary which will 1) provide for a dialogue in regard to the child's progress in reading books at home and at school; and 2) be a means of parents informing the school about any other literacy activities in which the child has been involved, e.g. joining a book club, writing a story at home, reading captions in the supermarket.

MATHEMATICAL AREA OF LEARNING

A broad and appropriate mathematics curriculum for young children can contribute to their overall development. The nurturing of positive attitudes from the start to learning mathematics is arguably even more important than teaching competencies.

The new NC orders for KS1 involve three attainment targets: using and applying mathematics; number; and shape, space and measures. All these are appropriate to include in a prestatutory curriculum and are considered below. However, although there is a body of knowledge that young children should start to acquire, most importantly young children should feel competent and confident as mathematicians. For this reason, the use and application of mathematics must be regarded as the most important element.

Shape, space and measures

Arguably, in everyday lives people find that their spatial awareness and understanding of measurement is even more important than numeracy. The child's earliest experiences are concerned with space, and positions in space and shape. Having had opportunities to move around in different spaces, to handle objects of different shapes and sizes and to fit them into spaces, by arranging and rearranging things, the child learns about distance. Gradually, and only after having gone through these active experiences, the child comes to understand about distance and the meanings of such terms as 'near' and 'far', 'in between' and 'behind'.

Through increasing knowledge of their own bodies, young children learn different ways of fitting in and moving in space. Older and more mature children will begin to understand the invariance of space; they will realise that a large piece of pastry remains the same even if it is divided into small pieces among a group. Having had a broad experience of different shapes, children will learn shape names initially for two-dimensional objects and then move on to three dimensions. As well as learning the names of shapes, children will come to understand the characteristics of different shapes and learn to make comparisons.

As the child becomes aware of shapes in everyday life from an early age, he or she will come to recognise patterns and relationships: as the child begins to think logically, he or she starts to distinguish differences and similarities in things and will arrange them in order. Given the opportunity, the child will show a developing understanding of pattern through discussion, painting and printing, and through making patterns with blocks, beads and in model making. When making patterns children will use prediction, classification and sequencing skills.

In order for young children to learn how to measure accurately, they need many experiences in making judgements about amounts. The experiences should be with weight, length, distance, time, area and capacity, and this will lead to the use and understanding of comparative language. As understanding grows, children may go on to investigate the relationship between height and weight. If this parcel is the largest, does it mean that it is the heaviest?

Initially, children will have difficulty in understanding invariance of distance. They may believe that the distance between two places changes depending on the speed of travel or the direction in which one is travelling. Other judgements may be affected by size: a taller person may be considered older than a shorter person. At the time this thinking is quite consistent, and 'explanations' of the 'correct' answer will not be effective. Understanding will only come through exposure to relevant experiences and the opportunity to reflect with others on what this means. When listening to the child's comparisons and questioning about the reasons for his or her decisions, the teacher can follow this progress.

Number

Numeracy is often regarded by parents to be the only element in the early years mathematics curriculum and even in recent years this has been echoed by schools. During the first two years of the NC in primary schools, there was an over-heavy focus on numeracy and, in the third year of development, there remained a strong emphasis. OFSTED are also critical of the teaching approach being narrowed to the development of knowledge and the acquisition of pencil-and-paper skills: 'Too many [schools] did not pay sufficient attention to mental and calculator skills, to the development of understanding of to the use of the knowledge and skills in a variety of contexts.'[17]

If teachers of older pupils are being warned about this emphasis on paper-and-pencil work, the implications for teachers of reception children to encourage practical work are clear.

Cockcroft advised that schools should help children gain a 'feel' for number. It is perhaps not always appreciated that some young children arrive in school with this 'feel'. A person's capacity to perceive how many objects there are in a group without counting has been recognised for over 100 years. Kaufman *et. al.* termed this ability 'subtizing' and defined it as 'the rapid, accurate and confident reporting of the numerosity of arrangements of elements presented for short durations'.[18] Since then, studies have produced evidence to support that young children have been found to have a perceptual mechanism that enables them to recognise a number of objects up to 3 without having to label and count them.[19,20]

Further study of some of these children who had been found to be good 'subtizers' revealed that schools did not appear to recognise or use the knowledge that children had. Macmanara states that when some of the children had been in the reception class of one of the schools for some weeks, they started to count small sets in ones, when previously they had been able to 'subtize' the same size groups. This behaviour was re-enforced by the mathematics scheme of work used. Within a very brief period of time there was no evidence left that the children could identify the number in a group without counting.[21]

These findings alert teachers yet again to the importance of gaining a clear picture of what children can do, and also to recognise that their achievements may not necessarily be demonstrated in expected ways, in this case by counting. However, counting is now found to play an increasingly significant part in the early mathematics curriculum. Some years ago, Choat suggested that schools had a wrong emphasis: 'Time is devoted to getting young children to repeat the number names, mime the number sequence, and even draw the number symbols. Unfortunately, such activities have no bearing on a child's acquisition of mathematics or appreciation of the "numberness of number".'[22]

Although this statement was valid at the time, seventeen years later it must be critically reviewed in the light of considerable research which emphasises the importance of counting skills in learning number and also recognition of the child's early abilities in counting. Thompson uses a number of studies to conclude that many new entrants to school already possess a good intuitive understanding of some of the number concepts that the school will plan to teach them during their infant years. He suggests that this understanding includes having some abilities to:

recite a counting sequence to a required number in the right order; matching number names in one-to-one correspondence with objects which are counted; point at objects whilst reciting the number names; ensure that the same number name is not matched to two different objects; being able to understand the cardinal aspect of number.[23]

Thompson further suggests that although young children do have difficulties in showing a secure knowledge of the invariance of number in some grouping tasks, they demonstrate an implicit understanding of one-to-one correspondence by being able to count accurately. From this it may be that children who fail in a number-conservation task may still have a concept of number which is sufficient to cope with early computation.

The place of traditional aspects of prenumber activity, such as sorting and matching as a prerequisite for counting abilities, is also being seriously questioned. Some evidence points to young children being able to count collections of different objects and that this ability is not dependent on them perceiving the objects to be different.[24] Moreover, other studies suggest that helping children to match objects together, such as plates to knives and people to chairs, does not necessarily help them to pair a number name with an object.[25]

Although these somewhat controversial findings will need to be carefully considered when reviewing classroom practice, the implications are that counting needs to assume a more central place in the reception class than perhaps it has done in the past.

In extending the child's 'feel' for number, there should be many opportunities for the child to develop a confidence in making his or her own judgements and so become more competent in making those judgements. At first the young child's 'best guesses' about a number of items may be random and way off the mark. Increased experience will result in more accurate responses. Through having many opportunities to estimate and offer approximations and to match these against what is counted or measured, children will come to a better understanding about quantity.

Although we now recognise that drilling young children to copy number symbols does not enhance their understanding, Martin Hughes's well recognised work has enabled teachers to acknowledge that even 4-year-olds are capable of representing their own number symbols which they can still recognise after a week. He also found that this age-group was capable of understanding the use of symbols + and − under certain conditions, although they could not generalise that understanding.[26] These findings point to the value of teachers exploring children's understanding of number in an open-minded way.

Using and applying mathematics

Papert suggests that the fundamental difference between a mathematician and a young child learning mathematics is not to do with the amount of technical information the child has acquired but is linked with the mathematician's emphasis on practical activity which, he asserts, may not always be apparent in school.[27] This statement made 13 years ago sadly still applies to those schools where there is a belief that the recording of symbols is the primary requirement for young children to demonstrate progress in mathematics. The emphasis on the use and application of mathematics not only relates to the other two attainment targets but also accords with the learning needs of young children with the emphasis on practical and investigative work. OFSTED emphasise the importance of this work throughout primary schooling. HMI recommend that 'much more of the teaching needs to strike a balance between teaching pupils the knowledge and those skills essential to an understanding of number and teaching them how to use that knowledge and those skills to solve problems and think mathematically'.[28]

As with literacy, children will have considerable knowledge and experience of mathematics before coming to school. The teacher will want to find out about each child's competencies and understanding in order to build on this. We have seen in the previous section that children are already thinking mathematically when they come to school. However, their methods and strategies for learning will be individual. The teacher's task, as for literacy, is to find out what mathematical understanding the child has in order to build on this. As with other aspects of learning, mathematics is embedded in experiences, and related language is gradually learnt.

A facility with mathematical language does not necessarily mean that understanding is present. Nor will children learn merely by being presented with words. On the other hand, first-hand experiences are so important that children who have had opportunities to handle and manipulate real things may have considerable mathematical understanding, although they may not necessarily have the linguistic labels to attach to their knowledge. This emphasises the importance of teachers observing children's actions very closely, as well as listening to their language.[29]

The NCC suggested five main aims to be achieved in using and applying mathematics. These are to

1. develop problem-solving and investigational strategies;
2. develop mathematical concepts and techniques;
3. develop the ability to apply mathematics to a range of contexts;
4. develop a range of personal qualities; and
5. provide a sense of what mathematics is all about.[30]

These aims will best be met for young children through giving them opportunities to discuss their understandings, through encouraging them to apply these understandings in aspects of everyday life and through providing them with opportunities that invite them to investigate.

When using and applying mathematics, children are required to communicate to others what they know. This will involve them working together and engaging in discussions to find solutions to mathematical problems. When children share their mathematical discoveries, this helps the teacher to see the way in which they are thinking and also helps each child as he or she listens to others to begin to see how something may be viewed in a different way. However, it is necessary to be clear about what discussion involves. George Ball points out that 'in discussion people listen to one another and have the opportunity to contribute freely – there is not someone who evaluates and comments on everything that is said'.[31] He suggests features of good discussion include encouraging each child initially to make a statement about the nature of the task and then to share freely his or her perceptions of the problem. The teacher's main role is to listen, accept what is offered and seek some agreement from the group before he or she summarizes and clarifies the agreed statement. When the teacher positively responds to each child's mathematical insights, this encourages that individual to view his or her discoveries in a positive light and to regard the subject as pleasurable.

The school day offers a potentially rich source of mathematical experiences for children. They will use their mathematical knowledge when the teacher invites them to clear away and stack the blocks, matches individual children to chairs in the group, allocates a pencil to each child and finds out how many children can be comfortably accommodated on a circular carpet when listening to a story. The children may go on local outings where they look for patterns on the leaves in the park, count the number of letter boxes and red cars and, when back in the classroom, estimate how many conkers they have collected before counting them.

When children arrive in school they will use what they know about mathematics in play. Open-ended materials, such as sand and water, are particularly useful, and Gura emphasises that blocks also come into this category: 'The mathematical relationships of unit blocks are discovered by children in pursuit of their own creative ideas. This, coupled with their open-endedness puts unit blocks effectively in the category of "raw material"'.[32] Home play is also commonly used as a context for children to apply their knowledge of mathematics. However, contrary to conventional expectations, one small-scale study found that, despite the provision of appropriate props, young children did not tend to engage in mathematical experiences of setting the table, which involves sorting and matching one to one.[33] This study found that the most frequent mathematical activity was that of sharing, particularly the sharing of improvised food where even young nursery children demonstrated considerable knowledge of division.

Other observations of children's domestic play showed knowledge of shape, patterns, estimation and sequencing. These experiences were developed through play using pots and pans, making dough, play with washing and ironing, and measuring out food. In short, young children are often seen at their best when the mathematics they are required to do is seen to have a purpose.

Marion Bird, having worked extensively in mathematics with groups of 4- and 5-year-olds, is convinced that children do need the opportunity of being involved and taking their own initiatives in mathematical activity, rather than just passively receiving and learning mathematical facts. She continues to explain that, although the teacher might set up the mathematical activity such as pattern making, building towers or considering number sequences, the active participation should mean that the outcomes are dependent on what the children make of the activity. For example, when children were asked carefully to fix precut sticky shapes (circles, squares, triangles) on to individual outline drawings of a Christmas tree, they each produced very different arrangements which showed individual understandings of counting, shape recognition, structuring, classifying, sorting, decisions about inclusion/exclusion, patterning, equivalence, recognition of one-to-one correspondence, use of mathematical language and reasoning.[34]

This open activity contrasts starkly with a teacher-directed task when the children have only one way to respond and one correct answer to achieve. This type of 'closed' activity is still seen too often in commercial mathematics schemes. There is a very real danger that reception children (particularly the older and more able) are regarded as ready to embark on the initial stages of the main school scheme. Typically, initial recording activities in a scheme require children to 'draw two dogs' or 'colour in four fish'. Quite clearly these activities lack intellectual challenge and limit the scope for children to demonstrate their capabilities. Bird suggests that 'it is all too easy to make misguided assumptions as to what children will be able to do or not do; what they will need to practise; what they must do before they can cope with something else'.[35]

Suggested action

Headteacher and parents

- Invite parents of new children to a meeting entitled 'Is your child a mathematician?' This could explain the ways in which children's mathematical abilities are strengthened through practical and investigative work in school and suggest activity at home.
- Provide parents with a selection of booklets which enable them to see the potential for mathematics in everyday activity, e.g. 'Discovering maths in the supermarket' or 'Looking at numbers in the home'.
- Offer parents insights into what mathematics children are doing in school: display a week's programme in retrospect and highlight the mathematics learning involved.

Preschool groups

- Provide different experiences of shapes and sizes: hide an interesting-

Suggested Action contd.
shaped object in a string bag and encourage a small group of children
to feel it in turn and to try to guess what it is; initially the aim is simply
to offer many varied experiences; the next stage will be to encourage
the child to try to describe what he or she feels; some useful words
are thin, thick, curly, straight, narrow, wide, small, big – but it is
important to accept whatever descriptive words are offered.

- Check early counting skills: present a small group of children with
  a collection of five objects and ask them in turn to count them
  aloud; carefully observe (e.g. do they know number names? Can
  they recite number names sequentially? Do they match one object
  to each number?).

- Practise early counting: collect a range of stories and rhymes which
  emphasise number and offer these regularly, e.g. 'five little ducks',
  '1, 2, 3, 4, 5, once I caught a fish alive'; make a giant snakes and
  ladders game with numerals 1–10 and a large dice with numerals
  1–4 (duplicate numerals where necessary or include a '0'); play
  with only one or two children in order to maintain the pace of the
  game and offer each child plenty of matching and counting practice;
  require each player to describe the number on the dice and to count
  each move made.

Teachers and teaching assistants

- Find out about children's initial mathematical abilities and understandings of

  - mathematical language through use of large equipment and their
    response to invitations to 'go over, under, beside and between'
    pieces of apparatus;
  - numbers through requesting them to dial a specific telephone
    number and by providing a calculator, pad and pencil in the
    role-play area;
  - their strategies for addition by providing a small group with
    an interesting and relevant context and observing the reactions
    of each child, e.g Abdul's birthday party (provide photographs
    of individual children and an attractive picture of a birthday
    setting). 'It's Abdul's birthday party: he and his sister Shushka
    will be there and he has invited four other children (show
    photographs). Now, how many children will there be altogether

at the party?' Give each child the photographs to help him or her with calculating. You may find evidence of 1) counting the photographs from 1–6; 2) counting Abdul and Shushka as two and then counting on four others; 3) starting with the four guests and then counting on Abdul and Shushka; 4) use of fingers rather than photographs for counting (showing recognition that fingers can be a useful tool for calculating whatever the context and an important step towards disembedded learning); and 5) mental calculation (showing secure understanding of addition given these numbers and a further move towards abstract learning);

– conservation of number through playing a skittles game; use six plastic bottles, brightly coloured and weighed down with sand and a ball; ask the children 'how many skittles altogether? How many have you knocked down? How many are left?; arrange the bottles in different patterns; check which children recognise that, when two skittles are knocked down, the same number of skittles remains regardless of the spatial formation; and

– counting backwards: paint a number line outside (or on a rolled-up mat which can be used in the hall); play a hopping game when children are encouraged to count and hop forwards and backwards from 1 to 5 and then from 1 to 10.

• Analyse the potential for learning mathematics in your classroom activities; if necessary, make the provision more explicit, e.g. set up an opticians in your role-play area, complete with eye chart.
• Extract as much mathematics as possible from your fiction books; decide on a core of books which offer good mathematical value, e.g. *Rosie's Walk, Postman Pat* (positional language).

SCIENTIFIC AREA OF LEARNING

The non-statutory guidance produced to support NC science stressed that good science education helps the child to make sense of the world, and so is about active finding out.[36] This requirement remains evident in the revised curriculum requirements, and the purposes for the scientific area of learning are very clearly affirmed in the principles of early years practice described earlier in this chapter. The best start for science depends on children having plenty of things to explore and investigate, and also in teachers being aware of the scientific skills and understandings that may be developed.

The requirements for the KS1 programme of study ('Experimental and investigative science, life processes and living things, materials and their properties and physical processes') all have potential for good-quality early learning experiences. These are explored briefly here.

Children will experiment and investigate when they have the opportunity of working in depth with materials and are able to use them with confidence in trying out different structures. Gura describes children in the block project closely watching the effects of their own actions and the actions of others, and suggests that children initiate their own research into matters that interest them.[37] HMI describe one example when a group of 4-year-olds playing with blocks were guided into investigating the properties of different bondings. Children built different walls, tested their strength by pushing them with a broom head and then attempted to explain why some walls were stronger than others.[38] It may be at this stage that some children are ready to consider the notion of fair testing: how some variables must be controlled to make the test 'proper'.

There are endless opportunities for young children to explore living things. The ways in which they are helped to note similarities and differences between themselves and other class members should emphasise 'uniqueness' in a way which will strengthen individual self-esteem. Children's natural curiosity about minibeasts can lead to them setting up their own inquiries and making close observations. As children observe tiny creatures over a period of time, they start to make simple predictions about their habits and behaviour, and ask further questions. Roy Richards sees discussion of these questions as a valuable opportunity for inviting further investigation:

> The important thing is to pick out such questions in day-to-day living, to engineer situations where similar questions can occur or, sometimes, even to pose such questions deliberately. Then teacher and children can sit down together and devise ways of finding answers to the questions. This is the heart of the scientific method and one of the most difficult yet most rewarding aspects that children and adults have to indulge in.[39]

If children have had rich sensory experiences, this provides a sound foundation for them to discriminate and sort, and to become aware of the different properties of materials. By manipulating materials they will learn about forces. The reception classroom can provide many and varied opportunities for these experiences, and the teacher will ensure that scientific thinking is taking place. However, if the emphasis is to promote thinking, this means that the chore of written recording should be reduced to a minimum. When young children are required to write about a completed model or about the properties of water, this requirement to write becomes the major task: recall of the actual activity becomes hazy and their motivation for further inquiry is lessened. The most appropriate ways for young children to demonstrate knowledge and understanding is through showing and telling.

Suggested action

Teachers and teaching assistants

Experimental and investigative science

- Use stories as a means of conveying scientific ideas, e.g. *The Enormous Turnip* (forces and motion), *Titch* (Pat Hutchins) (life processes and living things).
- Encourage children to predict, e.g. use a small art easel as a flip chart and scribe the predictions of a small group of children before they start an investigation; use sequential story books or books with flaps to encourage children to predict what they will see when they turn the page or lift the flap.
- Build investigative thinking into daily discussion, e.g.'Steven thinks that the snow has melted because it's daytime; Sharon thinks it's because of the sun. I think that we have a problem here that we could investigate'.

Life processes and living things

- Develop miniature gardens: have a digging patch of earth and provide a rotting log near the classroom entrance to allow discovery and easy observation of minibeasts.

Materials and their properties

- Have a 'materials' table as a regular feature in your classroom; display examples of two different materials weekly and use these as a focus for discussion, e.g. what other examples of the same materials can be added to the display? Scribe for the children as they note the similarities and differences between the materials.
- Explore 'change' in materials through adding different substances to a tray of water, e.g. colour, perfume, ice cubes, washing-up liquid, oil and paint; encourage children to predict, hypothesise, question and describe what they see.

Physical processes

- Help children to gain a notion of light and dark by providing thick

---

Suggested Action contd.
curtains to 'black out' the home corner, together with a torch.
- Encourage observation through shadow play and making shadows on the wall. Ask children to change the shape of their shadows and to suggest how they do this.
- Have a display of shiny objects which reflect light, e.g. mirrors, metal surfaces, spoons, prisms: encourage children to observe their reflections and talk about what they find.

TECHNOLOGICAL AREA OF LEARNING

Design technology

The principles of technology expressed by the Design Council are 'to help children to understand the made environment; identify ways in which they affect it and it affects them and empower them to bring about positive change for themselves and others'.[40] Young children have always been natural designers and, way before the NC, teachers have provided opportunities for these talents through building, modelling, sticking, making and cooking. Design and technology activities allow children to be creative – within a defined task. They offer a good context for co-operative work and enable children to learn about the properties and uses of materials, and require them to make decisions about which tools and materials are appropriate for certain purposes. Some of these skills, attitudes and abilities will naturally develop as a result of the task. Others will initially depend on the skilled observation and subsequent intervention of the teacher to ensure that learning is taking place. Design and technology does link very closely with all other areas of learning, but the teacher needs to make specific provision for activity which promotes early designing and making skills and helps children to start to understand some of the factors which help them to succeed in their work. Four useful headings for this work are 'Observing and exploring', 'Developing spatial awareness', 'Working with materials' and 'Representing findings'.

The starting point for children to observe and explore materials and constructions will depend very much on the experiences they have already had at home or in preschool settings. Before children are able to describe materials or consider similarities and differences, they need to have had many and varied opportunities to look very carefully and handle materials and to listen to descriptive language. Some of this work is very effectively managed in small groups with a voluntary assistant, who has been carefully briefed about the aims of the activity.

The Design Council suggests that

> Building with construction equipment can enable a child to understand how the component parts of a structure begin to relate to each other in space. Ideas and plans can be investigated, tested, and adapted easily in a concrete way. Children are able to control the outcome of their actions, defining and redefining until satisfied with the final result.[41]

As well as encouraging children to play freely with construction equipment, structured group activity and related discussion can help them to consider shapes and sizes and how they inter-relate – to look at component parts and see how these parts are joined. When children work with materials they exercise their physical skills as well as their mathematical and aesthetic experiences. The more they know about the properties of materials, the better able they are to use this knowledge for their particular purposes.

Young children need a broad range of opportunities to communicate what they have experienced and understood. Through discussion and questioning they will learn to talk about their findings with increasing confidence, and other communication may be through paintings and drawings. However, some children will represent all they know through the construction or the model they have made. In these cases a request for other forms of representation may be unnecessary and unprofitable.

Information technology

Although, for the purposes of early years, design and information technology come under the same umbrella, the new orders have separated information technology into a subject in its own right, and so raised its status. It is important, however, to allow children to use control technology to support all areas of learning.

Even if children do not have a computer at home, they will arrive at school already familiar with many examples of control technology, including having seen microwave ovens, digital clocks and used remote control to switch on the television. With this background, they are likely to view experiences in school with information technology with confidence and enthusiasm. Janet Broom, in her useful, practical guide, states that 'The computer opens up a new world for young children. It is a versatile machine that can give them a chance to be creative, to think logically, to solve problems, to have deeper insights into the concepts that they are acquiring and it can do a great deal more'.[42]

The reception teacher does need to be clear in his or her aims for the children. The staff at Tenterfield Nursery School aimed for children to have an equal opportunity to become familiar and happy with computers; to use them as an alternative means for creative art or music; to re-enforce early literacy and numeracy concepts, such as size, number, left/right orientation; to improve hand/eye co-ordination; to encourage problem-solving strategies and logical thinking; to build up social skills and language development; to help extend children's concentration; and to foster imagination.[43]

The management of a computer needs to allow for adult supervised activity. The adult may introduce the child to a new program, teach keyboard skills and generally discuss the significance of what is on the screen. Having acquired a degree of competence, children also need opportunities to use the computer unaided. By using open-ended programs in this way, the computer becomes a further valuable tool for children to represent their understandings.

Programmable toys also play an important role in helping children to understand control technology. The Roamer is a programmable robot which can move in any direction and play musical notes. After allowing for necessary free exploration of a Roamer, the children can use it to respond to the teacher's directions and then, more importantly, to create their own routes.

Suggested action

Headteacher, parents and governors

- Help parents and governors to understand about the purposes of work in early technology: organise an evening to display examples of children's work in design technology (with notices itemising skills and concepts learnt); demonstrate use of computer software, including LOGO and use of Roamers; provide suggestions for parents to provide technological experiences for children at home, e.g. using the telephone, switching on the microwave; make requests for recyclable materials that parents might contribute to aid design technology in school.

Preschool groups

- Ensure that your children have a wide range of opportunities to learn and apply cutting and sticking skills: make it manageable, e.g. initially very young children will be more effective in tearing paper rather than trying to use scissors; check that scissors can cut the material provided (fabrics may need to be precut) and that there are scissors available for left-handed children.

Teachers and teaching assistants

- Use stories as starting points for design and information technology. Read

  - *The Little Red Hen*: suggest that the little hen needs a vehicle to carry the sacks of corn to the mill; provide three miniature sacks of corn for each pair of children; offer a range of materials for constructing the vehicle, e.g. wood, Lego, card, string;
  - *The Patchwork Quilt* by Valerie Flournoy: suggest that the children design their own quilts using a range of material scraps for a collage; each child can create his or her own story about where the pieces from the quilt came from;
  - *Jack and Beanstalk*: alter the end of the story so that the giant did cut down the beanstalk; how can Jack find a way of getting back to earth?
  - *Postman Pat*: suggest that children devise their own system of roads and use the Roamer as the postman's van to deliver letters at certain houses.

- Provide children with examples of control technology in play situations, e.g. in the home corner provide a digital clock, push-button telephone and calculator.

HUMAN AREA OF LEARNING

This area includes social learning and, of course, social development is implicit across the curriculum. However, as social learning was included in the chapter on personal development, it is not emphasised here. The human area of learning encompasses aspects of the NC subjects of history, geography and environmental education. As with other learning, though, it will only have meaning and relevance to the child if it links to his or her own experience and background.

Although elements of all the new orders for history are applicable to children of reception age, the main focus will be in developing some understandings about the past and how it differs from the present. The NCC INSET materials (some of which are still helpful) suggest the related concepts involved in developing a child's sense of time and chronology include

• the development of an increasing vocabulary connected with time;
• the ability to sequence, e.g. using stories, days of the week, months, pictures;
• the development of a sense of period, e.g. during granny's life; and
• the ability to understand change and continuity.[44]

Within the context of daily classroom life, early concepts about time passing and sequence can be introduced and discussed. Initially, references to time will be loose – 'yesterday', 'a long time ago,' – but (importantly) this establishes a notion of a time other than 'now'. Similarly, daily routines and story times are good contexts to develop understandings about sequence and changes. Use of the child's own life history is a particularly powerful way of ensuring active learning.

Young children are naturally curious about their locality and the different work that people do in the community. This interest forms the basis of early work in preparation for the geography programme of study.

The layout of the school provides the initial reference point for geographical learning. Planned outings will then familiarise children with landmarks beyond the school which can later be referred to in discussion or related to similar landmarks in stories. Teachers are also aware of the additional fund of travel experiences that some young children will bring with them to school and which should be used.

The development of geographical skills is also appropriate. Starting with three-dimensional representation, young children can learn about reference points and how they are linked in the locality. Watkin, referring to two-dimensional work, suggests that through 'picture maps' discussion can be centred around place-related vocabulary, particularly in regard to distance of journeys, direction, location and scale.[45] Some reception-age children will have difficulty in moving from three to two dimensions, and will need plenty of opportunities to work with playmats and miniature landmarks before they progress to interpret symbols.

A statement in the non-statutory guidance for environmental studies summarised the significance of this work, which is now included in the thematic study for geography: 'Never has there been a greater need for young people to be aware of the necessity to look after the environment. They are its custodians and will be responsible for the world in which, in turn, their children will grow up'.[46] Each school locality has plenty of potential for young children to develop early knowledge about the environment and to learn how to care for it.

Suggested action

Preschool groups

- Help the child develop a record of his or her immediate past history: just before they come to school, young children will enjoy working with an adult to compile a 'book' of illustrations and captions which give examples of the preschool activities and routines. This can usefully be brought to school as a reminder of 'what I did when I was at nursery'. In discussion with the teacher, the child can then compare some of the similarities and identify what changes have taken place now that he or she is 'grown up and at school'.

Teachers and teaching assistants

- Use books to help children develop their observational skills and to discover hidden images, and use positional language to describe their location, e.g. *Each Peach Pear Plum* (J. and A. Ahlberg), *Animalia* (Graeme Base).
- Provide large, well mounted photographs of items situated in different parts of the school, e.g. flowers in the hall, a noticeboard, a doorway; after discussing these with the children, send them in small groups with an adult to identify their location; ask them to describe the location on their return.
- Use visitors and artifacts to develop the notion of changed times, e.g. furnish an open-sided dolls' house with prewar equipment and furniture on one side and modern furniture on the other (the actual period is not so important as the distinct difference between items, e.g. cooking range and microwave).
- Organise a visit to 'Get to know about our beautiful world': using the assistance of teaching and voluntary assistants, plan a visit to the nearest park or green space; brief the adults to encourage children to observe, touch, smell and listen to all the things around them and for

---

Suggested Action contd.
each adult to note down children's comments; on the return to school, these notes can be used to help children recall their experiences and record them through drawing, painting and modelling.

AESTHETIC AND CREATIVE AREAS OF LEARNING

As children develop, they represent their experiences of life through what means they have. Art, craft, music, dance and drama offer major opportunities for children to express and develop their ideas through visual and auditory perceptions, and to use materials, media and techniques. Barnes stresses the importance of clarifying ideas: 'What might have been an incomplete inner vision can become clear for them to give meaning to what they encounter and can help to build up concepts of themselves in relation to the world. Nowhere is this more obvious than when young children cannot read or write'.[47] Although Barnes is referring to art, this also applies to music, dance and drama. One good reason for encompassing all four subjects under this area of learning is to stress their value as a means of communication: through using art, music, dance and drama to communicate, children will also be taught some of the necessary skills and be introduced to the work of great artists and musicians. The four subjects are of equal worth, although this section concentrates only on art and music; the prime source of drama for 4-year-olds is through role play, which has already been dealt with (see Chapter 4), and dance is referred to under the physical area of learning.

Initially, in art and craft children do need time to explore materials for themselves. Roy Prentice suggests that there is a clear link between art and play. Drawing on studies which liken play to an attitude and process, he gives attention to the common presence of uncertainty and the need for choice and risk-taking. Opportunities for self-directed activity in two and three-dimensional art work allow children to explore the potential of different materials to meet their creative purposes. Prentice also points out that, although one of the main purposes of art education is to extend and deepen young children's sensory awareness, it is important to remember that, as with play, they will arrive at school with an uneven background of these sensory experiences. This has important implications for teaching. While the 'painting area' is a common feature in most reception classes and time is regularly allotted for painting, the emphasis is still more on art as simply as recreation for young children rather than a central means of learning. Learning implies teaching but does not mean imposing. The teacher can, nevertheless, help the child to refine and extend his or her painting or craft representation by guiding, and by suggesting the following ways:

- By offering appropriate stimulus; this may be through provision of sensory experiences, through aiding memory or imagination, through provision of materials, through demonstrating a technique.
- By teaching the subskills of handling tools, mixing and managing materials.
- By question and comment, encouraging the child to talk through his or her activity.
- By encouraging the child to combine materials and link different ways of representing experiences.[48]

Children come into school from a very noisy world. Many will have been exposed to a diet of indiscriminate sound – of traffic, chatter and background music from the media. Initial moves in musical education will usefully start with helping them to isolate and listen to sounds and to learn to compare and contrast them. At the same time, they will be extending a repertoire of songs and rhymes, some of which they already know by heart from preschool.

Children can learn a great deal about tempo, duration and the dynamics of sound simply through listening to the way in which the teacher uses his or her voice, and by responding with their voices and with various parts of their bodies. They may move on to making home-made instruments and exploring the different sounds made with these and pieces of commercial percussion. Only after lots of opportunities to play with and discuss these instruments will children then feel able to use them to depict sound effects in a story or to represent the sound of some shared experience.

The second requirement in both the programmes of study for art and music (knowledge and understanding) suggests that children should be exposed to high-quality examples of work which will both assist and motivate them in their own creative development. A booklet, *Arts and Schools*, describes the range of enrichment for school that is not available from usual school resources. This includes contributions from artists, people in the theatre and musicians.[49] Although the case studies in the booklet refer to older age-groups, there is a strong case for the youngest children in school having a similar entitlement to such expertise. The most important factor is that the professional contributors should be able to relate to and communicate with young children, and so form a relationship which will encourage them to want to know more.

Teachers can also provide the resources which will aid knowledge and understanding through pictures and examples of beautiful crafts. A small-scale study on developing art appreciation with nursery children demonstrated that such work is not lost on young children. Through offering them opportunities to view and discuss a range of paintings from different periods and cultures, the researcher concluded that the children's own view of art was extended and offered a broader content for their own work.[50]

Given the time and resources, access to informed teacher guidance and some high-quality stimulus, this will unleash young children's creative abilities into, in Robin Tanner's words, 'making the ordinary and trivial arresting, moving and memorable'.[51]

Suggested action

Headteacher and parents/governors

- Help parents and governors to see the purpose and potential of this area of learning. Hold a creative/aesthetic celebration for a half day in each term. Invite a group of no more than 10 adults at a time; give parents good notice to enable them to make arrangements with child-minders or to change their shift at work. Prepare a brief introductory pamphlet which outlines the aims of creative and aesthetic learning and stresses that the purpose of the day is for parents to experience some of the work in the reception class and to share this with their children; where adults are asked to support activities, prepare cards outlining their role, including some points for discussion and possible questions to ask.
- Include some of the following elements:

  - A musical session where adults and children play simple rhythm and pulse games, sing some songs by heart (provide a song sheet if necessary) and respond to a story using home-made instruments.
  - Story stimulus followed by children, supported by adults, representing an aspect of the story and selecting from a choice of painting, printing or use of collage materials.
  - Teacher introduction to colour mixing; adults and children working together to create different shades and tones of colour.

Teachers and teaching assistants

- Allow children to work in depth:

  - Start with one of the four areas of stimulus mentioned above and talk about possible themes to develop in paint or through three-dimensional work.
  - Suggest that children will need to think very carefully about what they are going to do; introduce the use of a 'thinking cap' which each child can put on when he or she closes his or her eyes. Stress that the work may take a long time – it doesn't have to be finished by the end of the session.
  - Help children to reflect on the development of their work with you after a fairly short period of time; scribe notes as they indicate what they feel they have achieved and what they might do next.
  - Before the child tires, suggest that he or she leaves the work and returns to it later; attach your notes to the work, explaining that these will help you both to remember what was going to be the next step in development.

PHYSICAL AREA OF LEARNING

Because physical action is so central for a young child, the effects of learning and development through movement are particularly broad. There is a close link to a child's personal growth. Physical education is also the only subject in the NC that is exclusively concerned with the child's physical body. Because of this, it is essential that this area of learning is not neglected and that the curriculum offers a broad range of opportunities for exercise. Exercise will improve the cardiovascular system, and will strengthen children's bones and muscles and will underpin all aspects of body growth.

The programme of study for physical education which includes games, gymnastics and dance can be offered appropriately to 4-year-olds, and dance links closely with aesthetic and creative learning. Although the allocation of time for other areas of learning may be distributed unevenly during the foundation year, with perhaps a particular focus in one term, physical education is the exception. Young children in particular do need regular planned opportunities for exercise, and there should be provision for this at least three or four times a week. Where possible, the sessions should be of 20–30 minutes duration, excluding time for dressing and undressing. However, in cold weather when children are taken outside, it is preferable to consider two briefer periods of time.

A physical activity lesson, however sensitively managed, will involve a great deal of new learning for this age-group. Children will need time to accommodate to the procedures for removing their clothes and for working in large open spaces, such as the hall or playground, and for learning to respond to precise verbal instructions from the teacher. Wetton suggests that, initially, the three areas for the physical education could be merged in order to focus on helping children accommodate to these new experiences, and to familiarise them with the terminology used concerning different parts of the body, names of various pieces of equipment and the meanings of various actions. She also recommends that early lessons can be simplified by highlighting the loco-motor skills of walking, jogging, running, hopping, skipping and galloping.[52] As children gain confidence the different elements of the three core areas can be emphasised.

Games, both indoors and outside, should emphasise the element of fun and play rather than competition, which will come only too soon. Initially, games will be without equipment and will concentrate on children stopping and starting on instruction and beginning to understand and respond to spatial language concerned with games (for example, up, down, behind, above). Small apparatus can then be introduced, such as bean bags, hoops and balls. In order to avoid a superficial curriculum, children will need time to experiment with each piece of equipment in varying ways before being introduced to the next.

In gymnastics, children first need to explore the actions of their bodies. The eventual use of large apparatus should not be introduced too early and, when it is, it should be regarded as an extension of these movements experiences rather than a separate lesson. The apparatus will be carefully selected to support the aims of the lesson, and an integral part of the child's experience will be training in the handling and moving of equipment. Children are likely to have had previous informal experiences of dance through responding to music and action songs in preschool settings, and through play at home. This will be further developed by introducing them to other stimuli and discussing their responses. The teacher can offer a great deal just through using his or her voice; before children can respond to percussion, they should have the opportunity to use the instruments for themselves and discover the range of sounds. Rose suggests that music should be chosen for three purposes, namely, for different ways of travelling; to help develop particular qualities of movement, such as sudden, heavy, light; and, lastly, to create a mood or atmosphere.[53]

In addition to teacher-directed sessions, careful attention should be paid to the opportunities available for physical activity through self-chosen play. The increasing attention given to outside areas in many cases now offers climbing apparatus, planks and tree trunks for balancing and imaginative playground markings for co-operative games, as well as attractive seating areas where children can rest after vigorous activity. Chris Rose comments that 'through experiences with movement and play, young children mix with others. They observe other children's behaviour and reactions, discover how friendships are made, and gradually become aware of evolving relationships'.[54]

Suggested action

Headteacher and parents

- Make clear to parents the central importance of physical activity for young children: stress the need for children to have exercise during weekends.

- Parents may worry about their children doing PE outside in cold weather. Explain the purpose of this and discuss the appropriate clothes to wear. You may agree that tracksuits and plimsolls are more suitable for comfort although, where apparatus is used, trousers and skirts should be removed.

Teachers and teaching assistants

- Prepare your children for physical education: take children for preliminary visits to the hall prior to them using it for PE. If the hall is very large, consider initially partitioning off with a screen part of it for use; try to enlist some additional teaching or voluntary assistance for the first few sessions when children change for PE; time is very well spent with individuals and small groups helping them to be systematic in undressing and dressing. Play games which encourage children to listen carefully and to respond to instructions, e.g 'Grandmother's footsteps', 'Statues'. Use objects to help children appreciate the qualities

Suggested Action contd.
of movement, e.g. drop a heavy piece of wood and note how it thuds to the ground; inflate and deflate a balloon and note how it changes shape and how it gently and soundlessly floats to the ground.

REFERENCES

1. Kitson, N. (1994) Fantasy play: a case for adult intervention, in J. Moyles (ed.) *The Excellence of Play*. Open University Press, Milton Keynes.
2. OFSTED (1993) *The Teaching of Reading and Writing in Reception Classes and Year 1* (Ref. 391/93/NS). OFSTED, London.
3. Hall, N. (1994) Play, literacy and the role of the teacher, in Moyles (ed.) (1994) *op. cit.* (note 1).
4. Centre for Language in Primary Education (1991) *The Reading Book*. CLPE, London.
5. Holdaway, D. (1979) *The Foundations of Literacy*. Ashton Scholastic, London.
6. Bradley, L. (1989) Predicting learning disabilities, in J.J. Dumont and H. Nakken (eds) *Learning Disabilities: Cognitive, Social and Remedial Aspects*. Swets Publishing, Amsterdam.
7. SCAA (1994) *The National Curriculum Orders*. SCAA, London.
8. HMI (1993) *op. cit.* (note 2).
9. Meadows, S. and Cashdan, C. (1988) *Helping Children Learn*. David Fulton, London.
10. HMI (1993) *op. cit.* (note 2).
11. Hall, N. (ed.) (1989) *Writing with Reason*. Hodder & Stoughton, Sevenoaks, p. x.
12. Shearer, J. (1989) How much do children notice? in Hall, (ed.) (1989) *op. cit.* (note 11).
13. Browne, A. (1993) *Helping Children to Write*. Paul Chapman Publishing, London.
14. Whitehead, M. (1990) *Language and Literacy in the Early Years*. Paul Chapman Publishing, London.
15. Sassoon, R. (1990) *Handwriting: The Way to Teach it*. Stanley Thornes, Cheltenham.
16. Whitehead, M. (1994) Language development in the early years: more than National Curriculum English, p. 108, in G.N. Blenkin and A.V. Kelly (1994) *The National Curriculum and Early Learning*.
17. OFSTED (1993) *Mathematics, Key Stages 1, 2 and 3, Third Year 1991–2*. HMSO, London, para. 7.
18. Kaufman, E.L., Lord, M.W., Reese, T.W. and Wolkman, J. (1949) The discrimination of visual number, *American Journal of Psychology*, Vol. 62, pp. 498–525.
19. Gelman, R. and Gallistel, C.R. (1983) *The Child's Understanding of Number*.

Harvard University Press, Cambridge, Mass.; Schaeffer, B., Eggleston, V.H. and Scott, J.L. (1974) Number development in young children, *Cognitive Psychology*, Vol. 6, pp. 357–79.

20. Macmanara, E.A. (1990) Subitizing and addition of number in young children. Unpublished MEd dissertation, University of Leeds.
21. *Ibid.*
22. Choat, E. (1978) *Children's Acquisition of Mathematics*. NFER, Slough, p. 47.
23. Thompson, I. (1994) Early years mathematics: have we got it right? *Curriculum*, Vol. 15, no. 1, pp. 42–9.
24. Maclellan, E. (1993) The significance of counting, *Education 3–13*, Vol. 21, no. 3, pp. 18–21.
25. *Ibid.*
26. Hughes, M. (1986) *Children and Number: Difficulties in Learning Mathematics*. Basil Blackwell, Oxford.
27. Papert, S. (1981) Teaching children to be mathematicians versus teaching about mathematics, in A. Floyd (ed.) *Developing Mathematical Thinking*. Addison Wesley, in association with the Open University Press, London.
28. OFSTED (1993) *op. cit.* (note 17), para. 87.
29. Dorset County Council (1984) *Mathematics with the Youngest Children*. DCC, Dorchester.
30. National Curriculum Council (1992) *Using and Applying Mathematics, Book B: INSET Handbook for Key Stages 1–4*. NCC, York.
31. Ball, G., with the Lakatos Primary Mathematics Group (1990) *Talking and Learning: Primary Maths for the National Curriculum*. Simon & Schuster Education, London.
32. Gura, P. (1993) *Exploring Learning: Young Children and Blockplay*. Paul Chapman Publishing, London, p. 79.
33. Haworth, J., Desforges, A. and Orgill, D. (1992) Home sweet home corner, *Education 3–13*, Vol. 20, no. 1, p. 38.
34. Bird, M. (1991) *Mathematics for Young Children*. Routledge, London.
35. *Ibid.*, p. 10.
36. National Curriculum Council (1989) *Science Non-Statutory Guidance*. NCC, York.
37. Gura (1993) *op. cit.* (note 32).
38. HMI (1989) *Aspects of Primary Education: The Teaching and Learning of Science*. HMSO, London, para. 58.
39. Richards, R. (1988) Learning through science in the early years, in G.M. Blenkin and A.V. Kelly (eds) *Early Childhood Education*. Paul Chapman Publishing, London.
40. Young, N. (1991) *Signs of Design: The Early Years*. Design Council, London, p. 3.
41. *Ibid.*, p. 10.
42. Broom, J. (1991) *Young Children Using Computers*. British Association for Early Childhood Education, London, p. 2.
43. *Ibid.*
44. National Curriculum Council (1993) *Teaching History at Key Stage 1*. NCC, York.

45. Watkin, D.G. (1990) Pictures to plans: some early map work in the infant curriculum, *Early Years*, Vol. 11, no. 1, pp. 55–66.
46. National Curriculum Council (1990) *Non-Statutory Guidance 7: Environmental Education*. NCC, York, Foreword.
47. Barnes, R. (1987) *Teaching Art to Young Children 4–9*. Routledge, London, p. 1.
48. Dowling, M. (1992) *Education 3–5*. Paul Chapman Publishing, London.
49. DES/Office of Arts and Libraries (1991) *Arts and Schools*. HMSO, London.
50. Payne, M. (1990) Teaching art appreciation in the nursery school: its relevance for three and four year olds, *Early Development and Care*, Vol. 61, pp. 93–106.
51. Tanner, R. (1985) The way we have come. From a talk at the opening of the Arts Centre at Bishop Grosseteste College, Lincoln.
52. Wetton, P. (1993) Everybody active, *Child Education*, August, Vol. 70, p. 43.
53. Rose, C. (1989) Physical education for the early years of schooling, in A. Williams (ed.) *Issues in Physical Education for the Primary Years*. Falmer Press, Lewes.
54. *Ibid.*, ch. 3, p. 29.

7

FOLLOWING AND RESPONDING TO YOUNG CHILDREN'S PROGRESS

Despite the massive amount of interest generated recently, and time and energy invested in assessment and recording, there is nothing new about noting how children respond to teaching and noting the achievements they make. Good teachers have always been interested in how and what children learn, and have used some of that information to influence their practice. Some of the most evocative descriptions of children's learning have come from early years settings such as Susan Isaac's school at the Malting House, Cambridge[1] and, more recently, from Chris Athey's study of nursery children during the Froebel Early Learning Project.[2]

These observations have offered early years practitioners models of observation which illuminate aspects of children's minds in action. Other examples of effective observations include the model linked to the ILEA Reading Record.[3] However, these informative descriptions did not exist everywhere. Perhaps a more honest overview of assessment of young children in schools prior to the NC was that of piecemeal, variable, subjective and idiosyncratic practice, much of which existed in its own right, in that it was not acted upon.

The great furore which has surrounded the issue of assessment since the onset of the NC has, in many ways, not helped the cause. Government imperatives required teachers to make assessment more explicit and systematic. The insensitive pace of change, poor communications among government, local authorities and schools, and the consequent stress and pressure caused have resulted in teachers understandably regarding these requirements as a dictate for a mechanical process of measurement in which real children have little place. Blenkin and Kelly summarise some of these tensions: 'The National Curriculum, with its elaborate arrangements for assessment, has imposed a different assessment model on early education . . . one which is incremental, summative, externally directed and designed to measure rather than guide the performance of pupils, teachers and schools'.[4]

While we recognise these concerns, we stress again that the reception teacher is not party to statutory requirements until children are of statutory school age. Although the teacher should be clear about the type and form of assessment required of his or her colleagues in KS1, the teacher is primarily concerned with his or her children here and now. The reception teacher wants to offer the children the best possible start to their educational career, and he or she needs to know how assessment fits into these intentions.

PURPOSES OF ASSESSMENT

Throughout this book, the emphasis is on children's development and learning: this is the central concern of all teachers, but in particular the reception teacher who is dealing with children at such a formative time in their lives. The teacher's planning of content, decisions about daily routines, preparation of the environment and teaching styles are all focused towards promoting children's learning.

Following on from this, it is important that we recognise the very close link between assessment and learning. Drummond aptly describes assessment as 'observing children's learning, trying to understand it and putting our learning to good use'.[5] In trying to understand we must look at children's intentions. The focus must be both on how the child feels about learning and how he or she approaches and tackles an activity as well as what the child knows and can do. This means observing the child's levels of confidence and motivation and his or her cognitive learning style as carefully as his or her achievements. The total of information should provide the teacher with an agenda to plan for the child's further learning. In the full knowledge that children learn in different ways and at different rates, the reception teacher will use his or her assessments to provide for individual learning needs. Sharp and perceptive assessments about children's personal idiosyncrasies, their hopes and fears as well as their attainment are a further requirement for providing a good match of curriculum to their future learning.

When making judgements about the achievements of all children, the teacher will notice those children who have difficulties with learning. A further purpose of assessment is to scrutinise these children more closely in order to identify where they require additional assistance and, where necessary, to present a case for additional human or material resources. The scrutiny is founded on the belief that the child's early difficulties will quickly become compounded and eventually mean the child experiencing a spiral of failure: this might be avoided by early intervention. However, a study which investigated various schemes for screening children concludes that pinpointing of early difficulties is no sure way of predicting future learning problems. Despite this, the authors suggest that there remains a strong case for offering additional help for children who have particular needs.[6]

Assessment of learning also helps the teacher to evaluate his or her curriculum. The way in which the child responds as a learner and the progress the child makes offer important messages about the effectiveness of that teacher's practice. It is worrying that, when some young children do not understand what is being taught, they believe themselves to be culpable. The hard but important fact is that the onus is not on the child to try harder but on the teacher to find an alternative route to learning. Assessment helps an evaluative process 'that explores how well the practitioner has connected the content intended for learning with the child as active meaning maker.[7]

However hard teachers work together to plan and organise common provision of curriculum content, the curriculum they offer to their children may differ as it is heavily influenced by their own beliefs about learning and expectations of children. Even when these are acknowledged and discussed, there can be different understandings about similar aims. For instance, classroom practice which purports to encourage children to share their views openly and to work independently may look similar at one level, but the limited expectations of one teacher and the insightfulness of another may result in the reality of separate practices. However, if the curriculum is agreed between teachers and evaluated in the light of children's learning, there is more chance of sharing professional views and understandings at a deeper level which, in turn, will offer children more equal opportunities. Teaching can only be improved by learning from what we know about children learning.

As we have stressed, good teachers have always been self-critical. They can be helped in this by encouragement to reflect on their practice in a systematic way, to share their assessments of children's learning and review their curriculum in the light of this information. Their team deliberations should help to ensure a more consistent curriculum for children. Spodek summarises this approach: 'Ultimately, the evaluation of early childhood educational evaluation must rest on the degree to which we can help to improve the education of all children by what we come to know about the education of some children'.[8]

The third purpose of assessment is linked to the teacher's aims to offer children a continuous route for their learning. I previously touched on the potential discontinuities which exist between home and preschool settings and what children experience in school (Chapter 2). It is also unrealistic to expect that progress along the curriculum path in school will be uninterrupted.

Teachers have given a great deal of time and attention to promoting continuity in learning. However, as previously mentioned, the work has mainly centred on curriculum content (see Chapter 4). Planning through topics offers links in the various areas of learning. Topics may be carefully planned for nine terms to include the reception class and KS1 in order to ensure that the content for learning prior to and in the early stages of the NC is sensibly distributed, and that children are introduced to an incremental and progressive set of experiences. This work is valuable in that it encourages shared debate, shared agreements about content and may lead to the building up of an archive of resources to support these experiences.

Nevertheless, this work is only concerned with the continuity of the planned curriculum. Ultimately, the teacher is concerned with what the child has understood. The framework of content must be responsive to what has been received. Once the received learning is assessed, it may become apparent that some of the learning outcomes are unintended, as well as those for which the teacher has planned. For example, as a means of assessing Sian's use of oral language and her ability to sequence, the teacher requested her to recall the story of 'The Sleeping Beauty', which had been read to the group the previous day. In so doing the little girl embellished the story and revealed considerable understandings of chronology and ways of living long ago. It was subsequently revealed that she had visited a museum of domestic life with her dad the previous week. The pleasurable experiences and conversations following that visit were reflected in the story recall and contributed to the links made in the child's learning about history. The teacher's assessment revealed much more than she had anticipated; it resulted in her additionally planning to develop a table display of old household artifacts and to use this as a means of promoting observation and further discussion.

It is this full information that needs to be acted upon to foster continuity of learning. The teacher has both responsibility for planning and assessing the learning; there is also an agreed agenda of content. But it is the children's responses that will indicate how rapidly and by what means they move through this agenda.

If assessments of each child's learning are shared with, and acted on, by the child's receiving teacher, this should safeguard continuity of learning as well as curriculum.

Assessment is an important aspect of accountability and this can and should be considered in two ways. Teachers have a contractual accountability to their employers, who include their governors, the LEA and central government. These employers are increasingly concerned with looking at the notion of the 'value added' offered to children during their early years in school. The interest is increased by decisions that have to be made about admission dates to school and the resourcing that is made available for early entrants. These purposes are important, but there is a danger that such decisions require quantifiable data. Placing priority on obtaining these data may deflect from the other purposes of assessment to improve teaching and learning.

Teachers are also professionally accountable to the families they serve. Parents not only have a right to know how their children are developing and learning during these early months in school but also have a large part to play in the process.

Teachers are finally answerable to the children, who need to be helped to see how and why they are progressing, in order for them to learn to help themselves.

In summary, then, assessment can help in the decisions made about policies and resourcing for young children; it can assist teachers to plan for consistent and continuous learning, and to reflect on and, where necessary, adapt the curriculum they offer. Assessment requires teachers to accept their contractual and professional responsibilities. Above all, assessment of children's learning should help the teacher to minimise the gaps which will always exist between the planned and documented curriculum that he or she intends to offer: the one that the teacher actually offers in the classroom and the curriculum the children receive.

ASSESSMENT ON ENTRY TO SCHOOL

So far we have considered assessment in a general way. Now we turn

to the assessment which particularly concerns the child's first teacher –
namely, the judgements which inform practice during the initial months
in school.

Schools have always had ways of finding out about children when they
start school. This was sometimes totally dependent on the reception teacher
discovering by trial and error the wealth of individuality within his or her
classroom. However, sometime before the NC there were considerable
moves on the part of schools and LEAs to establish some systems for
noting children's abilities on admission. A great deal of this early activity
was limited to gaining a summative picture of the child or, as Caroline
Gipps and colleagues describe, as a 'detection strategy'.[9]

Interest in 'detecting' where the child is increased with the introduction
of the NC: much of the activity sprang from a concern to establish a
starting point or base-line for what is added and eventually achieved in
the NC levels at year 2. The work is contentious and there are very real
fears about a type of assessment which aims to measure a child's ability
on entry to school. These fears are to do with the inappropriateness of
testing young children; the possibility of early 'labelling' of individuals;
implying judgements on parents as a result of measuring their children's
early achievements; the dangers of bias and discrimination; limiting the
assessment of children to that which is easily measurable; and promoting
a 'test' which is simply a logical down extension of NC assessment at
7 years.

Although standardised testing of young children is generally recognised
as inappropriate, criterion-referenced assessment gained in popularity.
Many base-line assessments still consist of schedules for teachers to use
with parents and for them to use in classrooms. Children's abilities are thus
checked against a discrete set of items. In some cases these schedules are
compartmentalised into discrete areas to identify early mathematical and
linguistic achievement. However, the items considered are often subskills
which are easily measurable. For example, the child's knowledge of shape
may be carefully checked whereas the over-riding question is concerned
with his or her spatial understandings. Desmond Nuttall summarises the
problem: 'there is a great danger of fragmentation into discrete objectives,
often low level because they are the easiest to specify, with the loss of
high level and integrating objectives'.[10]

The opponents of a summative base-line assessment advocate an
approach which Wolfendale suggests presents a '"rich picture" of the
child, expressive of the dynamic nature of development in the early
years'.[11] This approach, which is typified in the PROCESS assessment

materials developed by Merton LEA and Roehampton Institute of Higher Education, is grounded in open-ended child observations which initially aim to describe children's behaviour and achievements rather than evaluate it. This practice can be criticised on grounds of reliability, particularly in gaining a balanced picture of the child. For instance, Blatchford and Cline suggest that 'highlighting rare occurrences may provide a dramatic but possibly misleading picture, whereas noting more common but less striking behaviours might produce a more reliable account'.[12]

The two approaches view young children's early abilities very differently, which may be crudely summarised as judgemental and developmental. The summative base-line approach clearly acknowledges the different starting point of children when they start school. This approach draws on research such as the inner-London study of children's educational progress during their primary years.[13] This found that children's knowledge of reading, writing and mathematics on entry to school varied widely and was linked to their later attainments both at the end of the reception year and also three years after starting school. Following on from this, Blatchford's two longitudinal studies showed that children's reading-related knowledge when entering school correlated with their reading ability both at 7 and 11 years.[14] Although these findings need to be interpreted with caution, they indicate that young children arrive at school differently equipped to succeed, and that they maintain this equipment during their primary schooling. As Blatchford and Cline suggest, a systematic assessment procedure will help teachers 'to plan the delivery of the curriculum more carefully to respond to the needs of individual children and will make it less likely that schooling simply reinforces, by default, knowledge differences already developed and evident when children are first admitted'.[15]

By contrast, where the emphasis is on descriptive observations, although the individuality of children is fully recognised, there is a reluctance to view these individuals as being differently equipped as learners. For instance, in the introduction to the PROCESS assessment pack, Steirer suggests that 'if some children are deemed "not yet ready" to benefit from school the problem lies with an over-narrow definition of what schooling comprises rather than with a deficiency in the child'.[16] This strongly and properly supports the argument for a broad curriculum which will reflect many aspects of achievement. However, although reception teachers recognise the need to focus on and reflect children's strengths, they also need to concentrate on the areas that need developing. This surely implies the need for a sensitive but effective means of identifying what these areas are.

It is not helpful to polarise approaches, and I want to present a case for balance. Terminology is important, however, and the use of the term 'entry profile' best describes the suggested approach to initial assessment. The approach is based on particular characteristics of early years assessment and on the implications arising from these characteristics.

CHARACTERISTICS OF EARLY YEARS ASSESSMENT

Assessment is a demanding activity for the teacher of any age-group, but the assessment of young children is particularly complex and the reasons for this need to be examined.

Sound acquisition of new learning is always based on what we know already, and our confidence to move one step further into the unknown. Sound teaching is dependent on the teacher having made an assessment of what has previously been learnt. The reception teacher, unlike teachers of other age-groups, deals with children who have probably not received a common past experience. I have stressed throughout how much all children will have learnt before they come to school, but the range of experience and means of learning are likely to have been very different. The teacher's formidable task is to try to identify all that has touched each child in these early years, and to judge how this has affected the child's learning and competencies: evidence and assessment of this diversity provides the bedrock for the start of each child's school curriculum.

If we accept that learning is founded on previous experience, this leads to new learning being built on positive attributes – what is already known. It is too easy for the adult who does not have knowledge of early years to see young children's learning as deficient. The child's necessarily limited experience of life means that there are gaps in understanding which they plug with their own logic and so create something that they can understand – their own meaning. When assessing children's learning it is essential that the adult is able to give full credit, not only to what is known but also to those strategies used by the child to make meaning.

All learning is personal to the individual. We all have our different ways of learning, and some people certainly find learning easier than others. However, the learning of young children is both personal and private. The teacher of a 9-year-old may look at his or her writing and make some judgements about the child's grammatical skills, repertoire of expressive language and ability to structure and sequence narrative. If the pupil is demonstrably not understanding reflective symmetry, the teacher will encourage him or her to explain his or her particular difficulties. The answers to the teacher's questions may be hesitant and partial, but pieced together they form an agenda of evidence for the assessment. The evidence for assessing young children's capabilities and potential for learning is abundant, but it is more difficult to capture. It is patently not sufficient to rely on the symbolic representations that young children produce as evidence of what they know and can do, and even the most mature 4-year-old will have great difficulty in explaining his or her problems in learning. The great skills of the early years teacher is in helping children to reveal their learning.

The learning of young children is not only concerned with intellectual development. It is also broad and linked to all aspects of development. We have already explored the close links between the child's affective and cognitive growth. The ways in which children develop physically and use their bodies in making discoveries and refining their skills also has a marked effect on what is eventually achieved. The observations and judgements about learning must encompass a view of the child's total development as a person.

Learning is not neat and regular, even for adults. We struggle with some concepts, and forget parts of others, as well as finding some learning quite straightforward. For young children there is so much more to learn. Rates of development and learning are at their most rapid during these years, but the process of understanding also involves a piecing together of experiences, some of which may be partial and incomplete. Those who assess young children know too well that progress in education for young children is not linear. They recognise that the rate and pace of learning for individuals will differ, that sometimes it is untidy and that some children appear to take one step forward and two back along the road towards the NC.

IMPLICATIONS FOR ASSESSMENT OF YOUNG CHILDREN

We will consider the above characteristics in turn in trying to answer the question of what is required to create high-quality assessments which support children's learning.

Finding out about previous learning

Initially this means finding ways of identifying and making judgements about all that children bring to school with them. If teachers are to cue in to the child's previous learning and experience and start from where the child is, they need to find out what has happened during those very early years and the effect that this has had on each individual. The enormity of this task is obvious and, in order to make any useful progress, teachers must commit themselves to systematically piecing fragments of information together.

The main source of information will be the parents or whoever has primary responsibility for care of the child: however, other preschool personnel will play an important role. The preadmission contacts and initial weeks in school will offer teachers, teaching assistants and other members of the school community opportunities to gather further evidence. All this evidence, when analysed, will contribute towards a three-dimensional view of each child as he or she embarks on his or her educational career.

The central role that parents play in the education of their children is closely linked with the insights that parents have about their children as people and as learners. Teachers may be cautious about using this information, arguing that it is likely to be biased and partial. However, we are not looking at the information from parents to mirror teacher observations but should recognise the great value of receiving a subjective view of the child from persons who have had ongoing and intimate acquaintance with him or her. This information can highlight children's behaviour in different settings and throw light on a completely different world of learning at home. It can complement the information gathered by professionals and contribute towards a three-dimensional view of an individual. Hurst rightly suggests that teachers are very dependent on parents for this initial assessment.[17]

The climate in school must be such that parents are willing to share these insights they have about their children with teachers. In order for this to happen, parents must be convinced that their knowledge of their child is not only valuable but also a key ingredient for the school in order to help the child to progress.

It has already been suggested that the initial first visit to school can include opportunities for parents to talk freely about their child (see Chapter 2). However, that first meeting will need to cover a number of other issues and so may not be the most appropriate time to gather information for assessment. This first meeting is also likely to be with the head, whereas the reception teacher is really the key person to receive this information for assessment purposes. The PROCESS project on profiling in the early years specifically recommends that these meetings, which are designed for teachers to receive information from parents, should be targeted and carefully planned. The project suggests a conversational framework for parental discussions, in which the teacher introduces the purpose of the meeting, encourages the parents to talk freely about their child and then offers a summary of points made.[18] It is very helpful for teachers to start with such a framework, particularly if they feel tentative and ill-equipped to lead such a discussion. However, although good preparation and helpful guidance, such as that indicated, may give teachers necessary confidence, the key ingredient to a successful meeting will be the teacher's evident and genuine interest in what makes that child 'tick'.

Most children, by the time they are 4 years of age, will have attended some preschool setting; information about their behaviour and achievements in this setting can prove very useful to the teacher. Whatever the setting, it will probably have involved the child in making the first transition from home into a group. On that level alone it is helpful to know how that separation from home was achieved. However, after that, the great variation in preschool settings makes it impossible to have any standard expectations of the experiences offered or the benefits accrued. The Rumbold Committee stated that 'Children are affected by the context in which learning takes place, the people involved in it, and the values and beliefs which are embedded in it'.[19] These effects are very noticeable indeed when we look at a group of new entrants to school, some of whom may have attended a day nursery run by social services, while others may have had placements at a community playgroup, a private kindergarten, a local state nursery school or have stayed with childminders. Earlier in the book we looked at the potential discontinuities experienced by children when moving from one of these settings to school (see Chapter 2). Now, in the context of assessment, we look more closely at the effect of all that has happened in the preschool setting on the child's personal development and learning. Whatever the experience, it will have a formative effect on what happens to the child in school. As such, any information gathered about each preschool setting is valuable. It will help the teacher to see how budding dispositions and competencies of children have been nurtured or, sadly in some settings, how they have been inhibited and stifled.

Regardless of the quality of accommodation, where a child has had experience of a relaxed and unpressurised social setting, in which he or she has been valued as an individual, supported to achieve high standards in learning and self-discipline, it is highly likely that the child will arrive in the reception class as a confident and well motivated pupil.

The staff in a preschool setting will have acquired a great deal of information about the child which can be usefully shared. In the past there was often reticence from preschool personnel to offer this knowledge, largely because of confusions arising over the nature of the information required. The information was regarded as confidential and there was concern that it might be partial and prejudice the receiving teacher. However, unlike the partial perceptions received from parents, the preschool comments need to reflect factual evidence. If a child has been in a setting for 5–6 hours a week over a period of a year or more, the evidence collected about his or her development will be considerable: it is a wasted resource if this is not shared.

Building on positive factors

Tina Bruce stresses that, when assessing learning, what is important is to recognise what a child can do rather than what he or she cannot do.[20] This important principle immediately emphasises the need for a skilled early years practitioner whose knowledge of child development allows him or her to recognise just how much is being achieved. Parents are often unable to understand the significance of their child's actions, although intuitively they know that he or she is trying to make sense.

It is important for the teacher to know how to look at the world through the eyes of a child in order to appreciate that child's underlying intentions behind a decision or action. Vygotsky's statement made more than 50 years ago is still very relevant: 'It is not sufficient to understand his words – we must also understand his thoughts. But even that is not enough – we must also know its motivation. No analysis of an utterance is complete until that plane is reached'.[21] This implies a certain level of scrutiny. A single observation of a child's responses will provide a brief photograph of the here and now and a number of such observations will offer a more detailed picture. However, an in-depth judgement about a child requires a multilayered picture of activity which is developed over a period of time.

Some children will need to be observed particularly carefully. Young bilingual children who are at the early stages of learning English are a potentially vulnerable group. These children may be just as able linguistically as their peers. However, if they have had little experience of using English or seeing written English in the home, they are at a distinct disadvantage if their language and early reading and writing competencies are assessed on the same terms as those of monolingual children. If assessed in their home language, these children may also be penalised if they have not been supported in their home tongue in the classroom and so helped to acquire the language of the classroom and the curriculum. Gregory and Kelly outline the linguistic flexibility of bilingual children, including their creativity with words, in order to construct meaning. This, they suggest, is just one aspect of these children being aware of what they do not know and using language to find out.[22]

Fillmore suggests that a child will normally go through three stages in learning a second language. Initially, the child will develop social contacts with second-language speakers and rely heavily on body language and learning to recognise standard verbal cues and statements. Secondly, the child will start to use these cues and statements in order to communicate and, finally, he or she will refine the language used and concentrate on correctness. Fillmore also suggests that second-language learners use social contacts to support their learning by

- joining a group and pretending that they understand what is said even though this is not so;
- using a few learnt words to create the impression that they understand what is happening; and
- depending on friends for help.[23]

These stages of development and social strategies can be used as a means of assessing how the child is progressing in language acquisition and what means of support the child uses.

Helping young children to reveal their competencies

Children will only show us what they know and can do if they are given the opportunities to do so. This has very real implications for the classroom context for learning and the way in which the teacher spends his or her time. In looking at how we can best place the child in a position to reveal what he or she knows, six important factors emerge. These are that

1. children need to be given the appropriate means to express their understanding;
2. their thinking will be better applied if they are dealing with a familiar situation;
3. they will only fully show their abilities if they can make sense of the adults' intentions;
4. they need to understand the adult's use of language;

5. they will reveal their thoughts in conversations with adults and other children;
6. motivation plays a key role in encouraging children to use what they know.

Some of the studies which have developed Piaget's notions about young children's competencies are very relevant to these factors. One example is Piaget's three-sided mountain test which was discussed earlier (see Chapter 4). When children were required to recognise different perspectives within an unfamiliar setting, such as Piaget's Swiss Alps, they demonstrated very limited understanding. When given a more familiar home setting they were notably more successful. In a similar way we must recognise the difficulties that young children have in moving from their own first-hand learning to abstract and symbolic forms. Martin Hughes's work reminds us that children are able to demonstrate much deeper understanding than that revealed in their knowledge of mathematical symbols.[24]

In Chapter 4 we stressed the importance of children needing to understand a situation and making sense of the adult's purposes in order to succeed in making a response. In Piaget's well-known experiment on conservation, children stated that two sets of counters, when aligned, were the same, but when the second set of counters was pushed apart by the teacher, the children mainly considered that this second row contained more counters. In a modified version of this test, McGarrigle and Donaldson used a naughty teddy to push the counters apart and shuffle them around. This time more children gave the correct response than in the previous test.[25] Margaret Donaldson suggests that, in the first experiment, children considered that it made sense to believe that the teacher was acting purposively when pushing the counters apart, and this caused them to believe that, as a result, something different had occurred. With the introduction of a naughty teddy, the children were more likely to be open minded about the results of his actions.[26]

Understanding of the adult's spoken language is also important. Donaldson suggests that a young child may fail to carry out a task or respond inappropriately to a suggestion, not because the child is incapable but because the child cannot comprehend the language used.[27]

The central place of shared dialogue in developing learning has already been considered (see Chapter 4). Talking with and listening to children are also key methods of assessment. Drummond suggests that 'our attempts as teachers to get inside children's heads and understand their understandings, are enriched to the extent that children themselves are prepared to give us, through their talk, access to their thinking'.[28] This comment is a powerful reminder of the need for sensitivity in making the context for talk appropriate.

In the main, everyone works best at the things they like doing, and children are no exception. If young children are engaged in their learning they will demonstrate full use of their abilities in their urge to be successful. This emphasises the importance of providing children with intrinsically interesting activities and in providing a place in the curriculum for self-initiated activity.

Viewing the child as a whole

If we look at children's learning it is possible to see anything but not everything. Realistically, teachers must limit their observations: by allowing them to build up over a period of time they will be able to piece together fragments of behaviour, attitudes, approaches to learning and achievements. In total these will reveal a substantial portrait of each individual. It is also important to recognise that, if we wish to build up a composite picture of behaviour and learning, this may require different ways of assessing. This was acknowledged by a group of early years teachers in Dorset 13 years ago when they agreed that 'Appropriate assessment procedures need to be adapted for different areas of development, bearing in mind that part of a child's growth is intangible and difficult to measure'. They also recognised that 'Assessment . . . will vary according to the situation in which the child is working and the people with whom he or she is involved. Thus the context needs to be mentioned as part of the assessment'.[29]

A composite assessment requires the opportunity for the child to be observed in a variety of settings which, in turn, strengthens the case for a broad and interesting curriculum to provide these settings.

There is immense value to be gained from the detailed child observations made by a knowledgeable early years practitioner. These observations need to be planned, however, and some of the more recent assessment approaches which are based on observations (such as PROCESS and the Buckingham Observation Procedure (BOP)) emphasise the need for training in good observational techniques.

However, it is important to be clear about the most effective ways of gathering information about the child. Although well planned and sensitive observations reveal what a child is doing, it requires a different approach to reveal his or her capabilities and potential for development. A semi-structured situation needs to be set up in which the child can respond to a given situation. The setting for this should be as familiar as possible and the child must find the activity enjoyable.

Finally, the uncertainty surrounding some aspects of young children learning means that teachers must build confirmation into their assessment, sometimes backtracking, but always trying to ensure that the learning is secure and applied.

OVERALL AIMS OF AN ENTRY PROFILE

Two recent LEA surveys by Sheila Wolfendale revealed that individual schools consider an initial assessment of children to be a very important factor, although they are anxious to retain the responsibility for such procedures.[30] This is difficult to reconcile with any moves from government or LEAs to receive quantitative information about children which is based on standardised indicators. However, these schools are understandably putting the interests of their children first and want the freedom to decide on a system that will best meet their purposes.

The suggested approach in this chapter resists the idea of a simplistic way of measuring children's progress. There is, though, some merit in considering a system 'which assesses not the absolute levels of attainment of the children, but the progress they have made while under the influence of the school'.[31] This will be achieved most satisfactorily by gaining a clear and detailed picture of each child on entry; gathering a breadth of information about the child during his or her early months in school; and using a variety of assessment strategies for acquiring this information. The key elements suggested are close dialogue with parents and preschool educators, detailed and open-ended observations compiled by experienced early years practitioners, and use of carefully designed assessment tasks which children will enjoy tackling.

Above all, teachers will recognise the complexity of trying to gain a true and fair picture of a child at 4 years. In the end, as David and Lewis suggest, it comes down to our 'best guesses'.[32] However, we must ensure that these 'guesses' are in the hands of effective assessors, who know about young children's learning and who can move close to each child and recognise what is happening.

Priority must be given to making valid, rigorous and sensitive judgements about children's learning. The way in which these judgements are recorded and shared, although very important, is secondary. Nevertheless, recording and reporting measures should ensure that these judgements are used, in the child's interests, by teachers, assistants and parents.

Suggested action

Headteacher

- Arrange for all staff dealing with reception-age children to have refreshed insights into observing children; organise shared sessions for teachers, teaching assistants and supervisory assistants and local playgroup personnel; encourage shared observations of a sample of children during their last months in the playgroup and subsequently during their first term in school.

Teachers and teaching assistants

- Consider the different classroom contexts for assessment: note the routines and activities which are most likely to reveal different abilities and aspects of behaviour.
- Plan observations between you to cover a broad spectrum of activity over a period of time.
- Focus your observations occasionally on a particular disposition, e.g. children's sense of humour and how individuals use this as a coping strategy in school.
- Have brief but regular meetings to share and analyse these observations.
- Set up semi-structured tasks to assess the point of learning: use the materials that children are already playing with, e.g. use playmats, miniature cars, buildings and people as a means of assessing the child's understanding of shape in space, spatial language and jobs people do.
- Check that understanding is applied, e.g. if a child recognises different shapes and sizes of objects in the classroom, is this knowledge used in model making?
- Encourage children to share their perceptions of school, e.g. a teaching assistant in conversation with one or two children may be able to elicit valuable information particularly in relation to anxiety about school; conversational starters may include 'what is it like at this school? Is it as nice as playgroup? What do you tell mummy/daddy about what you do at school? Do you tell her/him

---

Suggested Action contd.
about anything that worries you about school, or things that you particularly like?'

- Help children to assess their own achievements, e.g. 'that model has taken you a long time, Sean. Is it the best one you have ever built? What was the most difficult part to do? Which part pleases you most?'
- Ensure that assessment results in action, e.g. having gained a rich picture of the child as a person, his or her learning dispositions and abilities in self-chosen and semi-structured tasks, it is helpful to review the action taken in regard to: the provision of different experiences; provision of equipment; use of adult time and intervention; and structuring of groups. Use your assessments to review provision for the class as a whole, e.g. look carefully at the ways in which your observations reflect the rich diversity of children in your class and check the ways in which your provision accommodates and supports this diversity.

Teachers and voluntary assistants

- Assessments are enhanced by the perceptions of voluntary assistants who work with small groups and individuals. However, this implies that they are aware of the need for confidentiality, which is stressed in the school's code of conduct (see Chapter 1). Provide helpers with pads of recording sheets and *aide-mémoires* for appropriate questions to ask or incidents to observe; emphasise that rough notes are perfectly acceptable but that it is important to note anything that surprises the helper; suggest a brief meeting after the lesson to share these jottings.

Teachers and parents

- Encourage parents to keep a note of the child's interests and experiences during the last months before coming to school; help parents to become aware of what reading, writing and numeracy takes place at home; ask them to bring to school any examples of early recordings of literacy and numeracy together with, or as an alternative, a painting, drawing or model that the child has recently completed (unaided if possible). Discussion of this work when the child starts school provides a good basis for initial conversations.
- Develop ways of keeping in touch with children's home life;

introduce a small posting box with pad and pencil; suggest
to parents that they use this to record details of any interesting incidents/activities which have affected their child at home;
hold regular but informal after-school sessions to receive this
information.

REFERENCES

1. Isaacs, S. (1930) *Intellectual Growth in Young Children.* Routledge & Kegan Paul, London.
2. Athey, C. (1990) *Young Children Learning.* Paul Chapman Publishing, London.
3. Centre for Language in Primary Education/Inner London Education Authority (1990) *The Primary Language Record. Handbook for Teachers.* CLPE, London.
4. Blenkin, G. and Kelly, A.V. (eds) (1992) *Assessment in Early Childhood Education.* Paul Chapman Publishing, London.
5. Drummond, M.J. (1993) *Assessing Children's Learning.* David Fulton, London, p. 13.
6. Lindsay, G.A. and Wedell, K. (1982) The early identification of educationally 'at risk' children revisited, *Journal of Learning Disabilities*, Vol. 15, no. 4, pp. 212–17.
7. Hurst, V. (1993) The implications of the National Curriculum for nursery education, in G. Blenkin and A.V. Kelly (eds) *The National Curriculum and Early Learning.* Paul Chapman Publishing, London, p. 55.
8. Spodek, B. (1982) Early childhood education: an overview, *Studies in Educational Evaluation*, Vol. 1.8, no. 3, p. 24.
9. Gipps, C., Steadman, S., Blackstone, T. and Stierer, B. (1983) *Testing Children: Standardised Testing in LEAs and Schools.* Heinemann, London, p. 62.
10. Nuttall, D. (1990) Unpublished discussion paper on National Curriculum assessment, Bera Policy Task Group on Assessment, p. 12.
11. Wolfendale, S. (1993) *Baseline Assessment: A Review of Current Practice, Issues and Strategies for Effective Implementation.* Trentham Books, Stoke-on-Trent, p. 29.
12. Blatchford, P. and Cline, T. (1992) Baseline assessment for school entrants, *Research Papers in Education*, Vol. 7, no. 3, pp. 247–69.
13. Tizard, B., Blatchford, P., Burke, J., Farquar, C. and Plewis, I. (1988) *Young Children at School in the Inner City.* Lawrence Erlbaum Associates, Hove and London.
14. Blatchford, P. (1990) Pre-school reading-related skills and later reading achievement; further evidence, *British Educational Research Journal*, Vol. 16, no. 4, pp. 425–8.
15. Blatchford and Cline (1992) *op. cit.* (note 12), p. 250.
16. Stierer, B., Devereux, J., Gifford, S., Laycock, E. and Yerbury, J. (1993)

Profiling, Recording and Observing: A Resource Pack for the Early Years. Routledge, London, pp. 4–5.
17. Hurst, V. (1991) *Planning for Early Learning: The Education of the Under-Fives.* Paul Chapman Publishing, London.
18. Steirer *et al.* (1993) *op. cit.* (note 16).
19. Department of Education and Science (1990) *Starting with Quality: Report of the Committee of Inquiry into the Educational Experiences Offered to Three- and Four-Year-Olds* (Rumbold Report). HMSO, London, paras 67–8.
20. Bruce, T. (1987) *Early Childhood Education.* Hodder & Stoughton, Sevenoaks.
21. Vygotsky, L.S. (1966) Play and its role in the mental development of the child, *Voprosy Psikhologii* (from a record of a lecture delivered in 1933).
22. Gregory, E. and Kelly, C. (1992) Bilingualism and assessment, in Blenkin and Kelly (eds) (1992) *op. cit.* (note 4).
23. Fillmore, L. (1976) The second time around: cognitive and social strategies in second language acquisition. PhD dissertation, Stanford University.
24. Hughes, M. (1983) What is difficult about learning arithmetic, in M. Donaldson (ed.) *Early Childhood Development and Education.* Basil Blackwell, Oxford.
25. McGarrigle, J. and Donaldson, M. (1974) Conservation accidents, *Cognition,* Vol. 3, pp. 341–50.
26. Donaldson, M. (1978) *Children's Minds.* Fontana, London.
27. *Ibid.*
28. Drummond (1993) *op. cit.* (note 5) p. 59.
29. Dorset Education Department (1982) *The Youngest Children in School.* DCC, Dorchester, p. 31.
30. Wolfendale, S. (1993) *Assessing Special Educational Needs.* Cassell, London.
31. Lindsay, G. (1993) Baseline assessment and special educational needs, in Wolfendale (ed.) (1993) *op. cit.* (note 30).
32. David, T. and Lewis, L. (1991) Assessment in the reception class, in L. Harding and J.R. Beech (eds) *Educational Assessment of the Primary School Child.* NFER/Nelson, Slough.

APPENDIX: HOME/SCHOOL AGREEMENT

RATIONALE

The child's admission to school offers a unique opportunity to establish a productive relationship between parents and teachers which is in the child's best interests. Such a relationship will be of greatest value if it is based on principles of equality and genuine mutual respect.

A 'signed understanding' between home and school helps to identify and clarify the position of each partner and signifies the importance of such a relationship.

Suggested approach

- Work with a small representative group of parents and governors (maximum of eight) to

  - discuss the merits of a home/school agreement; arrange for a key input followed by whole-group discussion; and
  - identify an initial list of the respective rights and responsibilities of parents and teachers; work in subgroups and arrange for each subgroup to consider this from the perspective of one of the partners; share findings and draw up a first draft.

- Circulate the first draft; discuss it at staff and governors' meetings; make it available at parents' meetings with a box for responses or include the draft in a letter to all parents.

Suggested Action contd.

• Adapt the document in the light of responses and produce a final copy to present at meetings for staff, parents and governors.
• Include copies of the agreement in your foundation year booklet for parents; discuss the booklet and arrange for joint signatures of the agreement at the meeting with new parents following their decision to send their child to your school; ensure that the agreement is seen as only part of the booklet, which will emphasise the significance of the induction to school and clearly describe the programme of work for the foundation year; ensure that both lists of responsibilities are discussed in order for parents fully to understand the intentions and required actions behind the wording; parents should feel secure that the agreement helps to affirm that education and care of young children is a job to be tackled co-operatively.

SUGGESTED MODEL AGREEMENT

Home/school agreement

To ensure that the foundation year offers (*name of child*) the best possible start to his or her schooling:

Parents' responsibilities

• To send your child to school regularly, on time, appropriately dressed, with necessary equipment clearly labelled and with lunch.
• Inform the school in writing if your child has been absent from school.
• To inform the school of any home circumstances which may affect the child's welfare and learning.
• To keep in touch with school events and, where practical, to attend meetings for parents which are organised for the benefit of your child.
• To help and encourage your child to learn at home as well as at school.
• Where family commitments allow, to support the running of the school by offering some of your time either to assist during school hours or to help with other functions out of school time.
• To communicate with the school if you are concerned that your child is not happy or is not making sufficient progress.
• To offer the school any personal insights or information about your

child which may help in making better provision for him or her in school.

Teachers' responsibilities

- To provide regular and frequent opportunities for discussion with you at the end of the school day and at monthly surgeries.
- To keep you informed through booklets, meetings and informal discussion groups about teaching and learning approaches which apply to your child during his or her first year in school.
- To communicate rapidly with you any concerns that the school might have about your child's happiness and welfare in school.
- To welcome any time or skills that you may be able to offer the school and to provide any necessary training workshops to support classroom work.
- To make available to you full information about how your child is progressing in school and to value your views about his or her development.
- To listen to any concerns that you may have about your child in school and to make clear the action that has been taken as a result of that concern.

Signed: *(parent)*

Signed: *(teacher)*

Date:

SUBJECT INDEX